Revealing & Healing

THE ISSUES OF THE HEART

Revealing & Healing

THE ISSUES OF THE HEART

DEVOTIONS & PRAYERS THAT ROOT OUT **30 SUBTLE SINS OF THE HEART** AND BRING HEALING TO YOUR SOUL

CLAYBORN & LAKESHIA MOMON

Copyright © 2025 Clayborn and Lakeshia Momon

All rights reserved.

No part of this book may be reproduced, scanned, or distributed in any printed or electronic form without permission. Please do not participate in or encourage piracy of copyrighted materials in violation of the author's rights. Purchase only authorized editions.

Unless otherwise noted, all Scripture quotations are taken from the New King James Version. Copyright 1982 © by Thomas Nelson. Used by permission. All rights reserved.

Table of Contents

Introduction

The Heart— The Wellspring of Life

The heart is more than just a physical organ that keeps us alive—it is the center of our emotions, desires, and spiritual well-being. It is the place where our thoughts, motives, and affections are formed. In Proverbs 4:23, we are given a clear directive: "Above all else, guard your heart, for everything you do flows from it." This verse is not just a gentle suggestion but a divine warning. The state of your heart determines the course of your life. What you allow to take root in your heart will shape your words, actions, relationships, and ultimately, your destiny.

But in today's world, our hearts are constantly under attack. We live in a culture that feeds us with messages of self-indulgence, comparison, bitterness, and pride. Social media fosters envy, relationships breed unforgiveness, and disappointments plant seeds of hopelessness. We find ourselves wounded by rejection, burdened by fear, and entangled in toxic emotions that distort our view of God, others, and ourselves. Many of us walk around with hidden pain, pretending to be whole while secretly battling jealousy, insecurity, anger, or even spiritual complacency. And over time, if left unchecked, these issues begin to harden our hearts, making it difficult to hear God's voice, receive His love, and walk in the freedom He desires for us.

This devotional is designed to take you on a journey of deep inner transformation. It is not just about behavior modification—it is about heart transformation. God desires to do more than just fix the symptoms of your struggles; He wants to go straight to the root and bring healing from the inside out. Throughout these pages, we will explore the hidden conditions of the heart—issues like pride, unforgiveness, fear, coveting, lust, and hopelessness. These are matters that, if left unchecked, will quietly poison our spiritual lives. But here is the good news: God is in the business of heart surgery.

One of the greatest lies the enemy tells us is that as long as we look good on the outside, we are fine on the inside. But Jesus made it clear that God is not concerned with outward appearances; He looks directly at the heart (1 Samuel 16:7). In Matthew 23:25-26, Jesus rebuked the religious leaders for appearing righteous while inwardly being full of greed and self-indulgence. This reminds us that real transformation does not happen through religious performance, good deeds, or public perception—it happens when we allow God to cleanse our hearts. Many of us have spent years managing symptoms, adjusting behaviors, and putting on masks, but true healing only comes when we allow God to deal with the root issues.

God does not expose areas of our hearts to condemn us—He reveals them so He can heal us. The Holy Spirit desires to uncover what we have suppressed, ignored, or accepted as "just the way we are." Maybe you've struggled with a hardened heart due to past betrayals, and forgiveness feels impossible. Maybe insecurity has paralyzed you, and self-doubt has shaped your identity more than God's truth has. Or maybe the pain of disappointment has caused you to lose hope, making you wonder if God even sees you. Whatever it is, the Lord is inviting you into a process of renewal, but the question is: Will you let Him in?

Ezekiel 36:26 declares, "I will give you a new heart and put a new spirit in you; I will remove from you your heart of stone and give you a heart of flesh." No matter how broken, hardened, or wounded your heart may be, God is able to restore it. He is the Master Potter who can take the shattered pieces of your life and create something beautiful. But this process requires surrender. It requires an openness to examine what's inside, to confront what needs to change, and to allow God to do the deep work within you.

As you go through this devotional, I challenge you to be honest with yourself and with God. Let Him reveal the hidden things in your heart. Let Him bring healing where there has been pain, conviction where there has been compromise, and renewal where there has been stagnation. Each day, as you meditate on His Word, invite the Holy Spirit to shape your heart to reflect His love, wisdom, and holiness.

This journey will not always be easy. There may be moments when the Word of God convicts you, when you feel the weight of the things you need to surrender. But don't resist the process—lean into it. Because on the other side of heart transformation is freedom. On the other side is peace. On the other side is a life fully surrendered to Christ, walking in the purpose and power He has called you to.

Are you ready to take this journey?

It's time to lay your heart before the Lord and allow Him to do what only He can do—make it new.

Let's begin.

In Christ,

Clayborn and Lakeshia Momon

1

Gossip – A Whisper That Wounds

"A perverse man stirs up conflict, and a gossip separates close friends." – Proverbs 16:28

REVEALING THE ISSUE

Gossip often begins subtly—a whispered comment, an innocent sharing of "concern"—but it can create significant damage. It sows seeds of discord, breaks trust and destroys relationships. Gossip thrives in the shadows, disguised as conversation, yet it is a tool the enemy uses to corrupt our hearts and hinder the unity God desires.

But why are we so tempted to gossip? At its root, gossip often stems from pride, insecurity, or a desire for attention. It's a reflection of an unhealed area of our heart, one that needs the transformative power of God's Word.

WHAT THE WORD SAYS

"Whoever keeps his mouth, and his tongue keeps himself out of trouble." – Proverbs 21:23

"Let no corrupting talk come out of your mouths, but only such as is good for building up, as fits the occasion, that it may give grace to those who hear." – Ephesians 4:29

God calls us to use our words to build up, not tear down. Gossip not only defiles others but also corrupts our hearts, as Jesus reminds us in Mark 7:20-23.

UPROOTING THE ISSUE

1. **Recognize Gossip:** Pay attention to the intention behind your words. Are they meant to build up or to tear down?

2. **Repent and Guard Your Heart:** Confess gossip to God and ask for His help in healing the insecurities or pride that fuel it.

3. **Redirect Conversations:** When gossip arises, resist the urge to contribute. Shift the focus to something uplifting. Be a peacemaker who points others toward Godly discussions.

4. **Speak Life:** Make it a habit to speak words of encouragement and truth. Pray Psalm 19:14: "May these words of my mouth and this meditation of my heart be pleasing in your sight, Lord, my Rock and my Redeemer."

5. **Consistently Pray for Others:** Make a practice of praying for others. When we make a habit to consistently pray for others, especially our enemies, with a genuine heart, it's hard to speak negatively about them.

HEALING PRAYER

Lord, I confess that I have used my words in ways that do not honor You. Some I may have spoken in ignorance, unaware that I was participating in gossip. I ask that you forgive me for any gossip I have spoken, and heal the brokenness in my heart that causes me to tear others down. Teach me to use my words for encouragement and truth, reflecting Your love and grace to everyone I encounter. Help me to be a vessel of peace and unity, for Your glory. In Jesus' name, Amen.

2

Competition – A Rivalry of the Heart

"Let us not become conceited, provoking one another, envying one another." – Galatians 5:26

REVEALING THE ISSUE

Competition can be healthy in certain contexts, like sports or professional growth, but when it becomes rooted in envy, pride, or a desire to outperform others for personal validation, it poisons the heart. This kind of unhealthy competition isn't about doing your best, it's about comparing, belittling, or elevating yourself above others.

At its core, unhealthy competition reflects a lack of trust in God's unique purpose and provision for each of us. Instead of celebrating the blessings and successes of others, it creates division, resentment, and an endless chase for validation through earthly achievements.

WHAT THE WORD SAYS

"Do nothing from selfish ambition or conceit, but in humility count others more significant than yourselves." – Philippians 2:3

"Each of you should use whatever gift you have received to serve others, as faithful stewards of God's grace in its various forms." – 1 Peter 4:10

God created each of us with unique gifts and callings. We are not in competition with one another but are called to work together to glorify Him. When we focus on comparison and rivalry, we miss the opportunity to fully walk in the purpose God has given us.

UPROOTING THE ISSUE

1. **Identify the Root:** Ask yourself, "Why do I feel the need to compete? Is it fear of being overlooked, pride, or envy?" Bring these struggles to God in prayer.

2. **Celebrate Others:** Choose to rejoice in the successes of others, trusting that God's blessings are abundant and not limited.

3. **Stay in Your Lane:** Focus on your God-given purpose, not someone else's. Meditate on Jeremiah 29:11, trusting that God has good plans specifically for you.

4. **Cultivate Humility:** Practice putting others first, as Philippians 2:3 teaches. Remember that God honors the humble and opposes the proud (James 4:6).

HEALING PRAYER

Father, please reveal any pride and/or envy in my heart that drives me to compete with others instead of trusting You. Help me to find my identity in You alone and not in how I compare to others. Teach me to celebrate the gifts and successes of those around me, and give me a humble heart that seeks to glorify You in all I do. Thank You for the unique purpose You have for my life. In Jesus' name, Amen.

3

Jealousy – The Poison of Comparison

"For where jealousy and selfish ambition exist, there will be disorder and every vile practice." – James 3:16

REVEALING THE ISSUE

Jealousy often starts as a fleeting thought: "Why them and not me?" But if left unchecked, it can take root in our hearts and grow into something toxic. Jealousy thrives on comparison, convincing us that God's blessings are scarce, and that others' successes are a threat to our own happiness.

Jealousy isn't just about wanting what someone else has—it's also about resenting them for having it. It causes us to view others as rivals instead of brothers and sisters in Christ. This can lead to bitterness, strained relationships, and even a distorted view of God. When we allow jealousy to guide our thoughts and actions, it reveals a deeper issue: a lack of trust in God's goodness and timing for our lives.

In the Bible, we see jealousy wreak havoc time and time again. Cain's jealousy led to murder (Genesis 4:1-8). Joseph's brothers sold him into slavery out of jealousy (Genesis 37:11-28). Even King Saul was consumed by jealousy of David, leading to a life of paranoia and destruction (1 Samuel 18:6-9). These examples show us that jealousy is a dangerous emotion that not only harms others but also eats away at our own peace and joy.

At its core, jealousy challenges the truth of God's character. It whispers lies that God isn't fair, that He's withholding good things from us, or that we are somehow less valuable than others. But God's Word assures us that His plans for each of us are good (Jeremiah 29:11) and that His blessings are abundant and overflowing (Ephesians 3:20).

WHAT THE WORD SAYS

"A tranquil heart gives life to the flesh, but envy makes the bones rot." – Proverbs 14:30

"Let us not become conceited, provoking one another, envying one another." – Galatians 5:26

"You desire and do not have, so you murder. You covet and cannot obtain, so you fight and quarrel. You do not have because you do not ask." – James 4:2

God calls us to shift our focus away from comparison and toward contentment. When we trust in His provision, we can be free from the bondage of jealousy and walk in peace and gratitude.

UPROOTING THE ISSUE

1. **Acknowledge the Feeling:** Be honest with God about your jealousy. Bring it to Him in prayer, confessing it as sin and asking for His help in overcoming it.

2. **Shift Your Perspective:** Remember that God has a unique plan for everyone. Meditate on Psalm 139:14, which reminds us that we are "fearfully and wonderfully made."

3. **Practice Gratitude:** Combat jealousy by thanking God daily for the blessings in your own life. Gratitude shifts our focus from what we

HEALING PRAYER

Heavenly Father, I surrender every jealous thought and envious feeling to You. Forgive me for comparing my life to others and doubting Your perfect plan for me. Help me to trust in Your timing and to celebrate the blessings You have given me. Fill my heart with contentment, gratitude, and peace, knowing that You have more than enough for all of us. Teach me to rejoice with those who rejoice and to walk confidently in the purpose You have for my life. In Jesus' name, Amen.

4

Assumption – Misjudging the Heart

"Do not judge by appearances, but judge with right judgment."
– John 7:24

REVEALING THE ISSUE

Assumptions are dangerous because they feel so natural. We often jump to conclusions based on limited information or personal bias. Whether it's assuming someone's intentions, motives, or circumstances, assumptions cloud our perception and lead to misunderstanding, conflict, and division.

At its core, assumption is rooted in pride. It says, "I already know," even when we don't have all the facts. Instead of seeking understanding, we rely on our own judgment, which is often flawed. This can lead to unjust accusations, broken relationships, and missed opportunities for grace.

Consider how assumptions played a role in biblical stories. Job's friends assumed his suffering was due to hidden sin, yet God rebuked them for their false judgment (Job 42:7). The Pharisee's assumed Jesus was blaspheming because they could not grasp His divine nature, leading them to reject the Savior. These examples show us how assumptions can blind us to truth and cause unnecessary harm.

When we assume, we take on a role that belongs to God alone—the role of Judge. But only God knows the thoughts and intentions of the heart (1 Samuel 16:7). Instead of assuming, God calls us to extend grace, seek understanding, and trust Him to reveal truth in His time.

WHAT THE WORD SAYS

"Fools find no pleasure in understanding but delight in airing their own opinions." – Proverbs 18:2

"Whoever guards his mouth preserves his life; he who opens wide his lips comes to ruin." – Proverbs 13:3

"Be quick to listen, slow to speak and slow to become angry." – James 1:19

These verses remind us that patience, understanding, and humility are essential to combat the temptation to assume.

UPROOTING THE ISSUE

1. **Pause and Reflect:** Before jumping to conclusions, pause and ask yourself, "Do I have all the facts? Am I making judgments based on appearances or incomplete information?"

2. **Seek Understanding:** Engage in conversations with a spirit of humility. Ask clarifying questions rather than relying on your own assumptions. Proverbs 18:13 says, "If one gives an answer before he hears, it is his folly and shame."

3. **Pray for Discernment:** Ask God for wisdom to see situations through His eyes, not your own. Remember, God's perspective is perfect, while ours is limited.

4. **Extend Grace:** Even when people's actions seem questionable, choose to extend grace instead of judgment. Be reminded of Jesus' words: "For in the same way you judge others, you will be judged" (Matthew 7:2).

HEALING PRAYER

Lord, I realize there are times when I rely on my own understanding instead of seeking the truth or trusting You. Forgive me for the times I've misjudged others and caused unnecessary hurt. Teach me to pause, listen, and approach every situation with humility and grace. Help me to see people as You see them, and to trust You as the ultimate Judge of all hearts. In Jesus' name, Amen.

5

Offense – The Trap That Steals Peace

"A person's wisdom yields patience; it is to one's glory to overlook an offense." – Proverbs 19:11

REVEALING THE ISSUE

Offense is like a trap carefully set to capture our hearts. It often starts small—a careless word, a misunderstanding, or unmet expectations. But when we hold on to offense, it begins to fester, creating bitterness, resentment, and division. Offense not only damages relationships but also robs us of the peace and joy God desires for our lives.

Jesus warned us about the inevitability of offense. In Luke 17:1, He said, "It is impossible that no offenses should come." Offenses will happen because we live in a broken, imperfect world. However, the true danger lies not in being offended, but in how we respond to it. Do we release it, or do we let it take root in our hearts?

Holding on to an offense often stems from pride or an unwillingness to extend grace. It blinds us to our own flaws while magnifying the faults of others. The enemy loves to use offense to divide families, friendships, and even the body of

Christ. Yet, Jesus modeled a different way—He forgave even as He hung on the cross, saying, "Father, forgive them, for they do not know what they are doing" (Luke 23:34).

When we hold on to offense, we choose bondage over freedom. Forgiveness, on the other hand, breaks the chains of offense and restores our peace. But forgiveness is not a feeling—it's a choice to trust God to handle the situation and bring healing in His way and time.

WHAT THE WORD SAYS

"Bear with each other and forgive one another if any of you has a grievance against someone. Forgive as the Lord forgave you." – Colossians 3:13

"Good sense makes one slow to anger, and it is his glory to overlook an offense." – Proverbs 19:11

"Be kind to one another, tenderhearted, forgiving one another, as God in Christ forgave you." – Ephesians 4:32

God's Word reminds us that forgiveness is not optional for believers. It's a command that sets us free from the prison of offense.

UPROOTING THE ISSUE

1. **Recognize the Trap:** Offense is a spiritual weapon the enemy uses to divide and distract us. Pray for discernment to see when offense is trying to take root in your heart.

2. **Examine Your Heart:** Ask yourself, "Why am I offended? Is it pride, unmet expectations, or a misunderstanding?" Bring your

feelings to God and allow Him to reveal any areas that need healing.

3. **Choose Forgiveness:** Forgiveness is a decision, not an emotion. Ask God for the strength to release the offense, trusting Him to bring justice and healing in His time.

4. **Seek Reconciliation:** When possible, have a conversation with the person who offended you. Approach them with humility and a desire for peace, as Matthew 18:15 instructs.

5. **Pray for the Offender:** This may be the hardest step, but it's the most freeing. Pray for those who hurt you, asking God to bless them and heal any brokenness in their hearts.

HEALING PRAYER

Father, I confess that at times I have allowed offense to take root in my heart. Forgive me for holding on to bitterness and resentment instead of trusting You. Help me to follow Your example of forgiveness and grace. Teach me to release offenses quickly and to guard my heart against the enemy's traps. May Your love and peace fill my heart, and may I walk in unity with others for Your glory. In Jesus' name, Amen.

6

Pride – The Root of All Sin

"Pride goes before destruction, and a haughty spirit before a fall." – Proverbs 16:18

REVEALING THE ISSUE

Pride is often called the root of all sin because it elevates self above God. It whispers, "I don't need help," "I know better," or "I can do this on my own." At its core, pride is a refusal to acknowledge our dependence on God and His sovereignty in our lives. It leads us to trust in our own strength, wisdom, and righteousness, rather than humbling ourselves before the Lord.

Pride can take many forms. Sometimes it's blatant arrogance, but other times it's more subtle, manifesting as self-reliance, perfectionism, or even a critical spirit. Pride often blinds us to our own flaws while making us quick to judge others. It disrupts relationships, fuels conflicts, and hardens our hearts to the truth of God's Word.

The Bible provides countless examples of the destruction caused by pride. Lucifer's pride led to his downfall (Isaiah 14:12-15). King Nebuchadnezzar boasted about his power and was humbled by God, living like an animal until he recognized God's sovereignty (Daniel 4:28-37). Even the Pharisees' pride in their own righteousness kept them from recognizing Jesus as the Messiah. Pride is a deceptive and destructive force, but God's Word offers a better way—the way of humility.

WHAT THE WORD SAYS

"God opposes the proud but shows favor to the humble." – James 4:6

"Humble yourselves before the Lord, and He will lift you up." – James 4:10

"Let the one who boasts, boast in the Lord." – 1 Corinthians 1:31

God calls us to humble ourselves, acknowledging that everything we have and everything we are comes from Him. True humility isn't about thinking less of ourselves; it's about thinking of ourselves less and exalting God above all.

UPROOTING THE ISSUE

1. **Acknowledge Your Pride:** Pride is often hard to recognize in ourselves. Ask the Holy Spirit to search your heart and reveal areas where pride may be lurking.

2. **Repent and Surrender:** Confess your pride to God, and surrender your need for control, recognition, or self-reliance. Trust that His plans and ways are higher than yours (Isaiah 55:8-9).

3. **Serve Others:** Pride focuses on self, but humility looks to the needs of others. Follow Jesus' example in Philippians 2:3-4, where we are called to consider others above ourselves.

4. **Stay Rooted in the Word:** Meditate on Scriptures about humility and God's greatness. Let His Word remind you daily of your dependence on Him.

5. **Boast in the Lord:** Redirect your focus to glorifying God, not yourself. Celebrate His goodness and faithfulness in your life rather than your own achievements.

HEALING PRAYER

Lord, please show me if pride has taken root in my heart. Please show me areas where I have relied on myself instead of trusting You. Forgive me for exalting my will above Yours and for thinking more highly of myself than I should. Teach me to walk in humility, acknowledging that every good thing comes from You. Help me to reflect Your love by serving others and glorifying You in all that I do. In Jesus' name, Amen.

7

Deceit – The Web of Lies

"The Lord detests lying lips, but He delights in people who are trustworthy." – Proverbs 12:22

REVEALING THE ISSUE

Deceit, whether through outright lies, exaggerations, or half-truths, is a direct assault on the character of God, who is the ultimate Truth (John 14:6). At its core, lying is about self-preservation or manipulation. We lie to protect ourselves, to avoid consequences, to gain an advantage, or to present an image of ourselves that isn't true. But deceit not only separates us from others—it separates us from God.

Lying may seem harmless at first, but it has far-reaching consequences. Each lie we tell builds upon another, creating a web of deceit that is difficult to escape. Lies destroy trust, damage relationships, and invite guilt and shame into our hearts. They are also a tool of the enemy. Jesus calls Satan the "father of lies" (John 8:44), reminding us that deceit is not just a bad habit—it's a reflection of spiritual bondage.

In the Bible, we see the destructive nature of deceit. Ananias and Sapphira lied to God and the apostles, which led to their sudden deaths as a judgment (Acts 5:1-11). Jacob deceived his father Isaac to steal Esau's blessing, creating years of conflict and separation within his family (Genesis 27). These stories remind us that deceit is not only sinful but also destructive to our souls, relationships and bloodline.

WHAT THE WORD SAYS

"Whoever walks in integrity walks securely, but he who makes his ways crooked will be found out." – Proverbs 10:9

"The truthful lip shall be established forever, but a lying tongue is but for a moment." – Proverbs 12:19

"Do not lie to each other, since you have taken off your old self with its practices and have put on the new self." – Colossians 3:9-10

God calls us to live lives of integrity, speaking truth in love and reflecting His character in our words. Lying may seem like an easy way out, but it ultimately leads to destruction. Truth, on the other hand, brings freedom and healing (John 8:32).

UPROOTING THE ISSUE

1. **Examine Your Heart:** Ask yourself why you feel the need to lie. Is it fear, insecurity, or pride? Bring these struggles to God in prayer, asking Him to reveal the root cause of deceit in your life.

2. **Confess and Repent:** Be honest with God about any lies you've told and seek His forgiveness. If your deceit has hurt someone, ask for their forgiveness as well.

3. **Commit to Truthfulness:** Practice speaking the truth, even when it's uncomfortable. Let your words reflect honesty, humility, and love.

4. **Guard Your Tongue:** Pray Psalm 141:3: "Set a guard over my mouth, Lord; keep watch over the door of my lips." Ask God to help you think before you speak.

5. **Walk in Integrity:** Remember that integrity builds trust and honors God. Strive to be the same person in private as you are in public, living a life that reflects the truth of the Gospel.

HEALING PRAYER

Lord, I confess that I have not always been truthful. Forgive me for the lies I have told and the ways I have been deceitful. Help me to walk in integrity, speaking truth in love and reflecting Your character in my words and actions. Teach me to trust in Your provision and protection, so I have no need to manipulate or deceive. Thank You for the freedom that comes through living in truth. In Jesus' name, Amen.

8

Foolishness – The Rejection of Wisdom

"The fear of the Lord is the beginning of knowledge; fools despise wisdom and instruction." – Proverbs 1:7

REVEALING THE ISSUE

Foolishness is not just about making mistakes or acting carelessly; it is a heart posture that rejects wisdom, discipline, and truth. At its root, foolishness is an attitude of pride and rebellion against God's guidance. It says, "I know better" or "I'll do it my way," disregarding the consequences.

The Bible describes the fool as someone who rejects God's authority, ignores correction, and lives for their own desires. Foolishness leads to impulsive decisions, sinful behavior, and spiritual blindness. It distracts us from God's purpose and prevents us from living a life that honors Him.

One of the most dangerous aspects of foolishness is its subtlety. It often hides behind worldly wisdom or popular culture, convincing us that we're right when we're actually far from God's truth. We see this in the parable of the foolish man who built his house on the sand (Matthew 7:24-27). Instead of grounding his life on the firm foundation of God's Word, he chose a path that seemed easier but ultimately led to destruction.

Foolishness also manifests in how we use our words and time. Proverbs 18:2 warns, "A fool takes no pleasure in understanding, but only in expressing his opinion." Similarly, Ephesians 5:15-16 calls us to make the most of our time, reminding us that foolish living wastes the precious opportunities God gives us.

Ultimately, foolishness is a rejection of the fear of the Lord—the reverence and awe of God that leads to wisdom and right living. Without this fear, we risk living according to our own understanding, which always leads us astray (Proverbs 3:5-6).

WHAT THE WORD SAYS

"The way of fools seems right to them, but the wise listen to advice." – Proverbs 12:15

"Whoever walks with the wise becomes wise, but the companion of fools will suffer harm." – Proverbs 13:20

"The fool says in his heart, 'There is no God.'" – Psalm 14:1

God's Word calls us to pursue wisdom, which begins with a deep respect and reverence for Him. Foolishness is the opposite of this pursuit, and it leads to spiritual, relational, and emotional destruction.

UPROOTING THE ISSUE

1. **Recognize Foolishness in Your Life:** Ask the Holy Spirit to reveal areas where you've acted foolishly—whether in your

decisions, relationships, or words. Humbly confess these areas to God.

2. **Seek Godly Wisdom:** Wisdom comes from God's Word and godly counsel. Surround yourself with people who encourage you to grow spiritually and challenge you to make wise choices (Proverbs 27:17).

3. **Practice Humility:** Be open to correction and willing to admit when you're wrong. Proverbs 9:9a says, "Instruct the wise and they will be even wiser,"

HEALING PRAYER

Father, I surrender my heart to You and ask for Your wisdom to guide my steps. Forgive me for any foolishness in my thoughts, words, or actions, and help me to walk in humility, seeking Your truth above my own understanding. Teach me to value wisdom, to embrace correction, and to build my life on the firm foundation of Your Word. Let my choices reflect reverence for You, and may my life bring You honor. In Jesus' name, Amen.

9

Division – Tearing What God Has Joined

"If a house is divided against itself, that house will not be able to stand." – Mark 3:25

REVEALING THE ISSUE

Division is one of the enemy's most effective tools to destroy relationships, families, churches, and communities. It often starts subtly—with differences of opinion, misunderstandings, or unmet expectations—but, if left unchecked, it grows into resentment, conflict, and brokenness. Division thrives when pride, selfishness, and unforgiveness rule the heart, preventing unity and peace.

The Bible emphasizes the importance of unity, especially among believers. Jesus prayed that His followers would be one, just as He and the Father are one (John 17:21). This unity is a reflection of God's love and a powerful witness to the world. Division, on the other hand, distorts this reflection and undermines the Gospel's message of reconciliation.

Division often arises from a refusal to extend grace or seek understanding. It can also stem from jealousy, gossip, or an unwillingness to humble ourselves in conflict. Paul addresses this in 1 Corinthians 1:10-13, where he rebukes the Corinthians for forming factions and identifying with different leaders instead of being united in Christ. This teaches us that division not only damages relationships but also dishonors God.

God calls us to guard against division by prioritizing love, humility, and forgiveness. Unity doesn't mean agreeing on everything, but it does mean valuing relationships over being right and pursuing peace even when it's difficult.

WHAT THE WORD SAYS

"Make every effort to keep the unity of the Spirit through the bond of peace." – Ephesians 4:3

"By this everyone will know that you are My disciples, if you love one another." – John 13:35

"Do not let any unwholesome talk come out of your mouths, but only what is helpful for building others up according to their needs." – Ephesians 4:29

God's Word reminds us that unity is a choice, and it requires effort, humility, and love. Division, on the other hand, is a result of the enemy's influence and the sinful desires of our hearts.

UPROOTING THE ISSUE

1. **Examine Your Role:** Ask yourself, "Have I contributed to division through gossip, pride, or unforgiveness?" Be honest with God and confess any actions or attitudes that have caused harm.

2. **Seek Reconciliation:** If you've had a conflict with someone, take the first step toward peace. Jesus teaches in Matthew 5:23-24 that reconciliation should be a priority in our worship and relationships.

3. **Choose Love Over Pride:** Division often thrives on pride and the desire to be right. Instead, choose humility and love, valuing relationships over winning arguments (Philippians 2:3-4).

4. **Pray for Unity:** Ask God to heal divisions in your relationships, church, or community. Pray for a spirit of peace and unity, trusting Him to bring reconciliation where it seems impossible.

5. **Commit to Building Others Up:** Replace divisive words or actions with encouragement and kindness. Speak life into others and look for opportunities to foster harmony.

HEALING PRAYER

Lord, reveal to me where I have allowed division to creep into my heart and relationships. Forgive me for the ways I have contributed to conflict or failed to pursue peace. Teach me to value unity and to love others as You have loved me. Help me to seek reconciliation, speak words of encouragement, and reflect Your heart for unity in all that I do. Heal any divisions in my relationships and within the body of Christ and let Your peace reign. In Jesus' name, Amen.

10

Manipulation – The Subtle Art of Control

"The integrity of the upright guides them, but the unfaithful are destroyed by their duplicity." – Proverbs 11

REVEALING THE ISSUE

Manipulation is a deceptive way of controlling others to achieve selfish desires. It often disguises itself as persuasion or concern but is rooted in dishonesty, pride, and a desire for power. When we manipulate, we use words, emotions, or actions to bend others to our will, prioritizing our agenda over truth and trust.

Manipulation is dangerous because it erodes relationships and dishonors God, who calls us to walk in integrity. Instead of trusting Him to provide and guide, manipulation takes matters into our own hands. It reflects a lack of faith and an unwillingness to let God work in His way and time.

The Bible provides clear warnings about manipulation. Delilah manipulated Samson into revealing the secret of his strength, leading to his downfall (Judges 16). Jacob manipulated Esau into selling his birthright and deceived Isaac to receive the blessing, creating years of strife in their family (Genesis 27). These stories reveal how manipulation harms relationships and distances us from God's will.

At its core, manipulation is a form of idolatry—it places our desires above God's authority and others' well-being. It's a subtle but destructive sin that often begins in the heart before manifesting in words or actions.

WHAT THE WORD SAYS

"Woe to those who draw sin along with cords of deceit, and wickedness as with cart ropes." – Isaiah 5:18

"Let your 'Yes' be 'Yes,' and your 'No,' 'No'; anything beyond this comes from the evil one." – Matthew 5:37

"The Lord detests lying lips, but He delights in people who are trustworthy." – Proverbs 12:22

God calls us to live in truth, sincerity, and humility, rejecting manipulation in all its forms. Honesty and trustworthiness reflect His character and allow us to build relationships that honor Him.

UPROOTING THE ISSUE

1. **Recognize Manipulative Behaviors:** Examine your actions and motives. Do you use guilt, flattery, or deception to get your way? Ask God to reveal any patterns of manipulation in your life.

2. **Repent and Seek Forgiveness:** Confess manipulation as sin and ask God for forgiveness. If your manipulation has hurt others, humble yourself and seek their forgiveness as well.

3. **Trust God's Plan:** Manipulation often stems from a lack of trust in God's timing and provision. Surrender your desires to Him, and trust that His plans are better than anything you can orchestrate (Proverbs 3:5-6).

4. **Commit to Integrity:** Speak truthfully and act with sincerity, even when it's difficult. Let your words and actions reflect honesty and humility.

5. **Pray for Wisdom:** Ask God to guide your interactions with others and help you rely on Him instead of resorting to manipulation. Pray for a heart that seeks His will above your own.

HEALING PRAYER

Father, I confess times or situations where I may have used manipulation to control situations and people, instead of trusting You. Forgive me for the times I've prioritized my desires over truth and integrity. Teach me to walk in humility and honesty, relying on Your perfect plan for my life. Help me to love others sincerely, reflecting Your character in my words and actions. Thank You for being trustworthy and faithful in every circumstance. In Jesus' name, Amen.

11

Control – Letting Go and Trusting God

"Trust in the Lord with all your heart and lean not on your own understanding; in all your ways submit to Him, and He will make your paths straight." – Proverbs 3:5-6

REVEALING THE ISSUE

Control is the desire to manage or dictate every aspect of life—our circumstances, relationships, and even outcomes. It often arises from a place of fear or insecurity, convincing us that if we don't take charge, everything will fall apart. While striving for control may seem responsible or necessary, at its core, it reveals a lack of trust in God's sovereignty.

The Bible warns us about the dangers of control. Adam and Eve sought control in the Garden of Eden, choosing to eat from the forbidden tree in an attempt to gain wisdom on their own terms (Genesis 3:1-6). Sarah, doubting God's promise, took matters into her own hands by urging Abraham to have a child with Hagar, leading to strife and division (Genesis 16:1-6). These examples show how the desire for control often leads to disobedience, brokenness, and chaos.

Control also distorts relationships. It can cause us to manipulate others, dominate situations, or refuse to delegate responsibilities. Instead of fostering trust and unity, it creates tension and resentment. Moreover, trying to control everything robs us of peace, as we carry burdens God never intended us to bear.

God calls us to surrender control to Him, trusting that He is in charge of every detail of our lives. When we let go of control, we make room for His power, wisdom, and grace to work on our behalf. True freedom is found not in holding on but in letting go and trusting God's perfect plan.

WHAT THE WORD SAYS

"Many are the plans in a person's heart, but it is the Lord's purpose that prevails." – Proverbs 19:21

"Be still, and know that I am God." – Psalm 46:10

"Humble yourselves, therefore, under God's mighty hand, that He may lift you up in due time. Cast all your anxiety on Him because He cares for you." – 1 Peter 5:6-7

These verses remind us that God's ways are higher than ours, and His plans are always for our good.

UPROOTING THE ISSUE

1. **Acknowledge Your Need for Control:** Be honest with yourself and God. Ask, "What areas of my life am I holding on to instead of trusting God?"

2. **Surrender in Prayer:** Bring your fears, plans, and desires to God. Pray, as Jesus did in the Garden of Gethsemane, "Not my will, but Yours be done" (Luke 22:42).

3. **Release Outcomes to God:** Trust that God's plans are better than yours, even when they don't align with your expectations. Meditate on Romans 8:28, which promises that God works all things for the good of those who love Him.

4. **Focus on Obedience, Not Control:** Instead of trying to manage every detail, focus on walking in obedience to God's Word. Let Him guide your steps.

5. **Cultivate Patience:** God's timing is often different from ours, but it is always perfect. Practice waiting on Him, trusting that He is working even when you can't see it.

HEALING PRAYER

Lord, I confess that sometimes I try to control situations and outcomes instead of trusting You. Forgive me for relying on my own understanding rather than submitting to Your will. Teach me to release my fears and desires into Your hands, knowing that You are sovereign and good. Help me to trust in Your plans and to walk in obedience, even when I don't have all the answers. Thank You for being a faithful and loving God who cares for every detail of my life. In Jesus' name, Amen.

12

Selfishness – Living for Me, Forgetting We

"Do nothing out of selfish ambition or vain conceit. Rather, in humility value others above yourselves, not looking to your own interests but each of you to the interests of others." – Philippians 2:3-4

REVEALING THE ISSUE

Selfishness is one of the most natural tendencies of the human heart. It prioritizes self above all else—our desires, comfort, and gain—at the expense of others. While the world often praises self-centered living as a sign of independence or self-care, selfishness is a subtle but dangerous issue that erodes relationships and distances us from God's will.

At its core, selfishness is a refusal to love sacrificially. It blinds us to the needs of others, hardens our hearts, and fosters a spirit of entitlement. This was evident in the rich man's story in Luke 12:16-21. He hoarded his wealth, building bigger barns to store it all, with no thought of using his resources to bless others or glorify God. In the end, his selfishness led to his eternal loss, as

God said to him, "This very night your life will be demanded from you."

Selfishness often shows up in subtle ways:

- Hoarding resources, time, or attention for ourselves.
- Ignoring the needs of others because we're too focused on our own priorities.
- Seeking recognition or glory instead of serving humbly.
- Resisting opportunities to give or sacrifice because of inconvenience.

These attitudes directly oppose the example Jesus set for us. He lived a life of complete selflessness, sacrificing His own comfort, reputation, and ultimately His life to serve and save humanity (Matthew 20:28). When we allow selfishness to rule our hearts, we miss opportunities to reflect His love and to experience the joy that comes from giving.

WHAT THE WORD SAYS

"For where you have envy and selfish ambition, there you find disorder and every evil practice." – James 3:16

"The generous will themselves be blessed, for they share their food with the poor." – Proverbs 22:9

"Whoever seeks to save his life will lose it, but whoever loses his life for My sake will save it." – Luke 9:24

Selfishness creates disorder and strife, but God calls us to a life of selflessness, where we find true joy, purpose, and peace in serving others and trusting Him to meet our needs.

UPROOTING THE ISSUE

1. **Examine Your Heart:** Take an honest inventory of your actions, thoughts, and priorities. Ask yourself, "Am I focused more on my own desires than on God's will or the needs of others?" Bring these struggles to God in prayer.

2. **Practice Gratitude:** Gratitude shifts your focus from what you lack to what you've been given. When you recognize how richly God has blessed you, it becomes easier to give generously and sacrificially.

3. **Serve Others Intentionally:** Look for ways to bless others, even when it's inconvenient. Volunteer your time, offer help to someone in need, or encourage someone who is struggling. Acts of selflessness grow a heart of humility and love.

4. **Give Without Strings Attached:** Whether it's your time, resources, or talents, give freely and joyfully, trusting that God will supply all your needs (Philippians 4:19).

5. **Pray for a Heart Like Jesus:** Jesus modeled perfect selflessness. Ask God to shape your heart to reflect His, enabling you to love sacrificially and live generously.

HEALING PRAYER

Father, help me to see where selfishness has taken root in my heart. Forgive me for prioritizing my desires above Your will and the needs of others. Teach me to live a life of humility and generosity, following the example of Jesus. Help me to serve selflessly, give generously, and love sacrificially. Shape my heart to reflect Yours, so that everything I do brings glory to Your name. In Jesus' name, Amen.

13

Stubbornness – Resisting God's Will

"Blessed are those who keep His statutes and seek Him with all their heart. They do no wrong but follow His ways." – Psalm 119:2-3

REVEALING THE ISSUE

Stubbornness often feels like strength. It can masquerade as determination or standing firm, but at its core, stubbornness is a refusal to yield—especially to God. When we resist His Word, His Spirit, or His plans, we place our will above His, shutting out the wisdom and guidance He longs to give us.

Stubbornness stems from pride and self-reliance. It says, "I know what's best" or "I don't need anyone's help." This attitude hardens our hearts and keeps us from experiencing the fullness of God's blessings. The Bible describes stubbornness as rebellion, equating it to idolatry (1 Samuel 15:23). Why? Because when we stubbornly cling to our own way, we exalt ourselves above God and make an idol of our desires.

The story of Pharaoh in Exodus illustrates the destructive nature of stubbornness. Time and again, God sent Moses to tell Pharaoh to release the Israelites, but Pharaoh's heart was hardened and he refused to submit to God's command. His stubbornness not only brought plagues upon Egypt but also led to his ultimate destruction (Exodus 7-14).

Stubbornness isn't just about refusing to listen to God—it also affects our relationships with others. When we refuse to admit we're wrong, listen to advice, or forgive, we create walls that prevent reconciliation and healing. Stubbornness isolates us and keeps us trapped in our own limited perspective, unable to grow or move forward.

WHAT THE WORD SAYS

"Do not be stiff-necked, as your ancestors were; submit to the Lord. Come to His sanctuary, which He has consecrated forever. Serve the Lord your God, so that His fierce anger will turn away from you." – 2 Chronicles 30:8

"A fool's way is right in his own eyes, but whoever listens to counsel is wise." – Proverbs 12:15

"Harden not your hearts, as in the rebellion." – Hebrews 3:15

God calls us to surrender our stubbornness, submit to His will, and trust in His plans. A tender heart that yields to God's guidance is one that He can shape and use for His glory.

UPROOTING THE ISSUE

1. **Recognize the Root of Stubbornness:** Ask yourself, "Why am I resistant to change or correction? Is it pride, fear, or mistrust in God?" Bring these underlying issues to God in prayer, asking for His help to soften your heart.

2. **Choose Humility**: Surrendering to God requires humility. Acknowledge that His ways are higher than yours (Isaiah 55:8-9) and remind yourself that submitting to Him is a sign of strength, not weakness.

3. **Seek God's Counsel:** Spend time in God's Word, allowing His truth to guide your decisions. Pray for wisdom and clarity and be open to the leading of the Holy Spirit.

4. **Be Open to Godly Correction**: God often speaks through others. Surround yourself with wise, godly people who can offer encouragement and correction, and be willing to listen with a teachable spirit (Proverbs 27:17).

5. Surrender Daily: Stubbornness isn't overcome overnight. Each day, surrender your plans, desires, and will to God, trusting Him to guide your steps.

HEALING PRAYER

Lord, I confess anywhere that I have allowed stubbornness to harden my heart. Forgive me for resisting Your will and placing my desires above Yours. Help me to walk in humility, surrendering to Your guidance and trusting in Your perfect plan. Soften my heart, Lord, and teach me to listen to Your Word, follow Your Spirit, and submit to Your ways. Thank You for Your patience and love as You shape me into the person You've called me to be. In Jesus' name, Amen.

14

Vanity – Chasing Empty Glory

"Charm is deceptive, and beauty is fleeting; but a woman who fears the Lord is to be praised." – Proverbs 31:30

REVEALING THE ISSUE

Vanity is an excessive focus on outward appearances, achievements, or approval from others. It's a trap that prioritizes what is temporary and fleeting over what is eternal and meaningful. In today's culture of self-promotion and social media, vanity often disguises itself as confidence, ambition, or self-care, but its root is a desire to glorify ourselves instead of God.

At its core, vanity is about placing our identity in the wrong things—our looks, possessions, talents, or status—rather than in who God says we are. It's a form of idolatry, exalting self-image and worldly validation above God's purpose for our lives. Vanity whispers, "If they admire me, I'll be worthy," but the truth is, our worth comes solely from being children of God, created in His image.

The Bible warns us about the emptiness of vanity. Ecclesiastes 1:2 declares, "Vanity of vanities! All is vanity!" King Solomon, the wisest man who ever lived, had wealth, wisdom, and fame, yet he recognized that these things could not satisfy the deepest longings of the heart. Vanity leads us to chase after things that cannot fulfill us, leaving us feeling empty and restless.

Vanity also distorts our relationships. It can lead to comparison, envy, and a critical spirit, as we measure ourselves and others by superficial standards. Instead of building others up, vanity turns our focus inward, making us overly concerned with how we're perceived rather than how we can serve and glorify God.

WHAT THE WORD SAYS

"Do not store up for yourselves treasures on earth, where moths and vermin destroy, and where thieves break in and steal. But store up for yourselves treasures in heaven." – Matthew 6:19-20

"For what does it profit a man to gain the whole world and forfeit his soul?" – Mark 8:36

Your beauty should not come from outward adornment, such as elaborate hairstyles and the wearing of gold jewelry or fine clothes. Rather, it should be that of your inner self, the unfading beauty of a gentle and quiet spirit, which is of great worth in God's sight." – 1 Peter 3:3-4

God calls us to look beyond the temporary and focus on what truly matters—our hearts, our character, and our relationship with Him. True beauty and worth come from a life that reflects His glory.

UPROOTING THE ISSUE

1. **Examine Your Heart**: Ask yourself, "What am I chasing? Am I seeking approval, admiration, or validation from others? Is my focus on outward appearances or worldly success?" Bring these questions to God in prayer, asking Him to reveal areas where vanity may be taking root.

2. **Shift Your Focus to God:** Instead of seeking to glorify yourself, seek to glorify God. Meditate on Psalm 115:1: "Not to us, Lord, not to us but to Your name be the glory."

3. **Cultivate Inner Beauty**: Focus on developing the fruit of the Spirit (Galatians 5:22-23) and growing in godly character. These qualities are far more valuable than outward appearance or accomplishments.

4. **Practice Gratitude:** Vanity often stems from discontentment. Combat this by thanking God for who He has made you to be and the unique gifts He has given you. Gratitude helps us find joy in Him rather than in worldly things.

5. **Serve Others Selflessly:** Vanity turns our attention inward, but serving others shifts our focus outward. Look for opportunities to bless and encourage others without expecting anything in return.

HEALING PRAYER

Lord, I surrender the areas where I have allowed vanity to take hold of my heart. Forgive me for seeking approval and validation from others instead of finding my worth in You. Teach me to focus on what truly matters—developing a heart that reflects Your love and truth. Help me to lay down my pride and self-centeredness, and to live for Your glory, not my own. Thank You for reminding me that my true beauty and value come from You. In Jesus' name, Amen.

15

Unforgiveness – The Poison That Corrupts the Heart

"For if you forgive other people when they sin against you, your heavenly Father will also forgive you. But if you do not forgive others their sins, your Father will not forgive your sins." – Matthew 6:14-15

REVEALING THE ISSUE

Unforgiveness is a silent killer. It doesn't just affect the person who refuses to forgive—it poisons their relationships, hinders their prayers, and even damages their health. Some people wear their unforgiveness like a badge of honor, believing that holding onto the offense keeps them in control. But the reality is, unforgiveness doesn't make you stronger—it makes you a prisoner.

Jesus made it clear that forgiveness is not optional. If we refuse to forgive others, we are cutting ourselves off from God's forgiveness (Matthew 6:15). This is because unforgiveness is rooted in pride—it says, "I have the right to hold onto this offense." But Jesus, who was betrayed, beaten, and crucified, looked down at His enemies and said, "Father, forgive them, for they do not know what they are doing" (Luke 23:34). If Christ could forgive in the midst of His suffering, how much more should we?

Unforgiveness is also a tool of the enemy. The devil thrives on division, bitterness, and broken relationships. Paul warns in 2 Corinthians 2:10-11 that when we refuse to forgive, we give Satan an advantage over us. The enemy loves to keep people bound in the past, reliving their pain, and replaying offenses over and over. But when you forgive, you break free from the enemy's grip and reclaim your joy and peace.

WHAT THE WORD SAYS

"Get rid of all bitterness, rage, and anger, brawling and slander, along with every form of malice. Be kind and compassionate to one another, forgiving each other, just as in Christ God forgave you." – Ephesians 4:31-32

"Bless those who curse you, pray for those who mistreat you." – Luke 6:28

"Love keeps no record of wrongs." – 1 Corinthians 13:5

UPROOTING THE ISSUE

1. **Release the Debt:** Forgiveness doesn't mean excusing what happened, but it does mean choosing to no longer hold it against the person. Let it go and trust God to be the judge.

2. **Pray for the Offender:** It may feel difficult at first, but praying for the person who hurt you softens your heart and allows healing to take place.

3. **Walk in Freedom:** Forgiveness isn't just about them—it's about you. Choosing to forgive releases you from the bondage of bitterness and positions you to receive God's best.

HEALING PRAYER

Heavenly Father, I release every grudge, every wound, and every person who has hurt me into Your hands. I refuse to let unforgiveness keep me in bondage. Teach me to forgive as You have forgiven me, to let go of the pain, and to walk in the freedom of Your grace. Soften my heart and help me love even those who have wronged me. In Jesus' name, Amen.

16

Vengefulness – The Burden of Retaliation

"Do not take revenge, my dear friends, but leave room for God's wrath, for it is written: 'It is mine to avenge; I will repay,' says the Lord." – Romans 12:19

REVEALING THE ISSUE

In keeping with the previous issue of Unforgiveness, vengeance is what begins to spring up when we don't forgive. Vengefulness is the desire to repay harm with harm, to take justice into our own hands when we feel wronged. It might come from a deep sense of betrayal, anger, or a longing to restore what was taken. At its root, however, vengefulness reflects a lack of trust in God's justice and an unwillingness to release our pain to Him.

The desire for revenge often feels justified. After all, the wrongs we've experienced may be real and painful. However, when we hold on to vengeful thoughts, we are the ones who suffer. Vengefulness hardens our hearts, fuels bitterness, and keeps us trapped in a cycle of anger and resentment. Instead of bringing resolution, it weighs us down with an unbearable burden that only God can lift.

The Bible offers us examples of vengefulness and its consequences. Cain, consumed by anger and jealousy, killed his brother Abel and bore the curse of his actions for the rest of his life (Genesis 4:1-16). King Saul, driven by vengeance and jealousy, relentlessly pursued David, leading to his own downfall (1 Samuel 18:6-11). These stories remind us that vengeance never brings peace—it only deepens the wounds we're trying to heal.

Jesus offers us a radically different approach: forgiveness. He tells us to love our enemies, to bless those who curse us, and to pray for those who persecute us (Matthew 5:44). On the cross, Jesus exemplified this by forgiving the very people who crucified Him, saying, "Father, forgive them, for they do not know what they are doing" (Luke 23:34).

WHAT THE WORD SAYS

"Do not repay anyone evil for evil. Be careful to do what is right in the eyes of everyone." – Romans 12:17

"Blessed are the peacemakers, for they will be called children of God." – Matthew 5:9

"Do not say, 'I'll pay you back for this wrong!' Wait for the Lord, and He will avenge you." – Proverbs 20:22

God's Word reminds us that vengeance belongs to Him alone. Our role is not to seek revenge but to trust His perfect justice and to walk in forgiveness and peace.

UPROOTING THE ISSUE

1. **Acknowledge Your Pain**: Vengefulness often comes from unresolved hurt. Take time to acknowledge the pain you've experienced and bring it to God in prayer. He cares deeply about your wounds and wants to bring healing.

2. **Surrender Your Desire for Revenge:** Release the need to take matters into your own hands. Pray Romans 12:19, trusting that God's justice is perfect and complete, even when it's not immediate.

3. **Choose Forgiveness:** Forgiveness doesn't mean excusing or forgetting what happened. It means releasing the offender into God's hands and freeing yourself from the chains of resentment.

4. **Pray for Those Who Hurt You**: This may feel impossible, but praying for those who wronged you is a powerful step toward healing. It aligns your heart with God's and opens the door for His peace to enter.

5. **Replace Vengeance with Love:** Look for ways to bless others, even when it's hard. Acts of love and kindness not only reflect God's character but also help to heal your heart.

HEALING PRAYER

Lord, I release all vengeful thoughts towards those who have wronged me. I repent for wanting to take justice into my own hands. Forgive me for the bitterness and anger I've allowed to take root in my heart. Help me to trust You as the righteous Judge, knowing that Your justice is perfect. Teach me to forgive as You have forgiven me, and to release the burden of vengeance into Your hands. Fill my heart with Your peace and help me to reflect Your love even to those who have hurt me. In Jesus' name, Amen.

17

Covetousness – The Silent Thief of Contentment

"You shall not covet your neighbor's house. You shall not covet your neighbor's wife, or his male or female servant, his ox or donkey, or anything that belongs to your neighbor." – Exodus 20:17

REVEALING THE ISSUE

Coveting is a heart condition that breeds discontentment, comparison, and jealousy. It's more than just wanting what someone else has—it's an unhealthy longing that can consume your thoughts, alter your perspective, and create bitterness toward God and others. It blinds us to our blessings because our focus shifts from gratitude to greed.

The world thrives on coveting. Social media, advertising, and even conversations with friends constantly expose us to what others have, subtly planting seeds of dissatisfaction in our hearts. You see someone with the dream job, the ideal relationship, the perfect body, or the lifestyle you wish you had, and suddenly, what God has given you seems insufficient. You begin asking,

"Why not me?" instead of thanking God for what He has already done.

Coveting is dangerous because it can lead to resentment toward God. When you feel like others are advancing while you are stuck, you might start to question His goodness and fairness. The Israelites did this when they compared their situation to Egypt, longing for what they left behind instead of trusting in God's provision (Numbers 11:4-6). Their covetousness led to complaining, which led to rebellion, which ultimately kept them wandering in the wilderness instead of entering the Promised Land.

At its root, coveting is idolatry—it places material things, relationships, and personal desires above God. Paul warns in Colossians 3:5, "Put to death, therefore, whatever belongs to your earthly nature… and greed, which is idolatry." When we covet, we shift our trust from God as our provider to our own desires as the source of our fulfillment.

WHAT THE WORD SAYS

"Keep your life free from love of money, and be content with what you have, for he has said, 'I will never leave you nor forsake you.'" – Hebrews 13:5

"Delight yourself in the Lord, and he will give you the desires of your heart." – Psalm 37:4

"Better a little with the fear of the Lord than great wealth with turmoil." – Proverbs 15:16

UPROOTING THE ISSUE

1. **Cultivate Gratitude:** The antidote to coveting is thankfulness. Daily reflect on God's blessings and acknowledge how far He has brought you.

2. **Renew Your Mind:** Comparison is a trap. Choose to focus on God's plan for your life rather than what He's doing for others. Your journey is uniquely designed for you.

3. **Trust God's Timing:** Coveting often stems from impatience. Instead of rushing ahead or becoming frustrated, remind yourself that God's timing is perfect. He knows exactly what you need and when you need it.

HEALING PRAYER

Father, I repent for any envy or coveting that has taken root in my heart. Help me to focus on the blessings You have given me instead of comparing myself to others. Teach me contentment and gratitude and remind me that my worth is found in You alone. May my heart always seek You first. In Jesus' name, Amen.

18

A Critical Spirit – Tearing Down Instead of Building Up

"Do not judge, or you too will be judged. For in the same way you judge others, you will be judged, and with the measure you use, it will be measured to you." – Matthew 7:1-2

REVEALING THE ISSUE

A critical spirit is a habit of finding fault, whether in others, ourselves, or circumstances. It often starts small—comments made in frustration or internal judgments—but can quickly grow into a mindset of negativity and condemnation. This attitude not only strains relationships but also grieves the heart of God, who calls us to love and encourage one another.

At its core, a critical spirit reflects pride and self-righteousness. It assumes, "I know better," or, "I would have done it differently." Instead of showing grace and understanding, it focuses on faults, often exaggerating them while ignoring the good. A critical spirit blinds us to God's work in others and creates division, bitterness, and even isolation.

The Bible gives sobering warnings about this behavior. The Pharisees were critical of Jesus, constantly finding fault with His actions and teachings, despite His sinless nature and divine authority. Their critical attitudes not only hardened their hearts but also blinded them to the truth of who He was. Similarly, in Numbers 12:1-10, Miriam and Aaron criticized Moses out of jealousy, and God rebuked them severely. These stories remind us that a critical spirit is not just harmful—it's a sign of rebellion against God's work in and through others.

WHAT THE WORD SAYS

"Do not let any unwholesome talk come out of your mouths, but only what is helpful for building others up according to their needs." – Ephesians 4:29

"Why do you see the speck that is in your brother's eye, but do not notice the log that is in your own eye?" – Matthew 7:3

"Encourage one another and build one another up, just as you are doing." – 1 Thessalonians 5:11

God calls us to speak words of life, not criticism, and to focus on lifting others up instead of tearing them down.

UPROOTING THE ISSUE

1. **Recognize the Root Cause**: A critical spirit often stems from pride, insecurity, or unresolved hurt. Ask God to reveal what's driving your critical thoughts and attitudes.

2. **Repent and Seek Forgiveness:** Confess your critical spirit to God and ask for His forgiveness. If your criticism has hurt others, seek their forgiveness as well.

3. **Practice Gratitude:** Shift your focus from faults to blessings. Make it a habit to thank God for the good in others and in your circumstances. Gratitude is a powerful antidote to negativity.

4. **Speak Life**: Commit to using your words to encourage and build up. Before speaking, ask yourself, "Will this bless, help, or uplift the person I'm speaking to?"

5. **Extend Grace**: Remember that everyone is a work in progress, just as you are. Instead of focusing on faults, pray for others and trust God to work in their lives.

6. **Guard Your Heart and Mind**: Meditate on Philippians 4:8, which calls us to focus on what is true, noble, right, pure, lovely, and admirable. Filling your mind with God's truth helps combat a critical spirit.

HEALING PRAYER

Lord, I ask you to reveal to me any areas where I have allowed a critical spirit to take place in my heart. Forgive me for focusing on the faults of others instead of seeing them through Your eyes of love and grace. Teach me to speak words of life and encouragement, and to extend the same grace to others that You have shown me. Help me to build up instead of tearing down.and to trust in Your work in others and in myself. Thank You for Your patience and mercy as You transform my heart. In Jesus' name, Amen.

19

Anger – Turning Fury into Freedom

"In your anger do not sin: Do not let the sun go down while you are still angry, and do not give the devil a foothold." – Ephesians 4:26-27

REVEALING THE ISSUE

Anger is a powerful emotion, and while it isn't inherently sinful, it can quickly lead to sin if left unchecked. Anger often arises when we feel wronged, disrespected, or out of control. At its core, anger demands justice—it insists that things should be made right, often on our terms.

However, when anger goes unresolved, it becomes destructive. It hardens our hearts, fuels bitterness, and damages our relationships with others and with God. The Bible warns that unchecked anger can give the enemy a foothold in our lives, allowing him to use our frustration to sow division, resentment, and even hatred.

Consider Cain's story in Genesis 4:1-8. Cain's anger toward his brother Abel led to murder because he allowed it to fester and control his actions. Similarly, King Saul's anger and jealousy toward David consumed him, driving him to disobedience, paranoia, and ultimately his downfall. These stories remind us that anger, when unchecked, has the power to destroy lives.

But anger doesn't always have to lead to destruction. The Bible shows that even Jesus experienced righteous anger, such as when He cleansed the temple of corruption (John 2:13-16). His anger was directed at injustice and was expressed in alignment with God's will. This example teaches us that anger itself isn't sinful—it's what we do with it that matters.

WHAT THE WORD SAYS

"A fool gives full vent to his spirit, but a wise man quietly holds it back." – Proverbs 29:11

"Refrain from anger and forsake wrath! Fret not yourself; it tends only to evil." – Psalm 37:8

"My dear brothers and sisters, take note of this: Everyone should be quick to listen, slow to speak and slow to become angry, because human anger does not produce the righteousness that God desires." – James 1:19-20

God's Word calls us to handle anger with wisdom and self-control, surrendering it to Him rather than allowing it to control us.

UPROOTING THE ISSUE

1. **Acknowledge Your Anger:** Don't deny or suppress your anger. Instead, bring it before God, honestly expressing your emotions in prayer. He already knows your heart and wants to help you process your feelings.

2. **Identify the Root Cause:** Ask yourself, "What's fueling my anger? Is it fear, pride, unmet expectations, or a sense of injustice?" Understanding the root helps you address the deeper issue.

3. **Pause Before Reacting**: When anger arises, take a step back. Pray, breathe, or count to ten before responding. Proverbs 15:1 reminds us that "a gentle answer turns away wrath."

4. **Surrender Your Anger to God:** Let go of the need to control or seek revenge. Trust God to handle the situation in His way and timing. Meditate on Romans 12:19, which says, "It is mine to avenge; I will repay," says the Lord.

5. **Pursue Peace and Reconciliation**: If your anger involves another person, seek reconciliation. Approach them with humility, express your feelings without blame, and work toward resolution as instructed in Matthew 18:15.

6. **Guard Against Bitterness**: Unresolved anger can turn into bitterness, which poisons the soul. Pray for the Holy Spirit to help you forgive and release any lingering resentment.

HEALING PRAYER

Lord, I surrender any anger that I may have allowed to take root in my heart. Forgive me for the ways I've let it control my actions and hurt others. Teach me to process my anger in a way that honors You, and help me to let go of any bitterness or desire for revenge. Fill me with Your peace and guide me to pursue reconciliation and forgiveness. Thank You for Your patience and for the power of the Holy Spirit to transform my heart. In Jesus' name, Amen.

20

Hopelessness – The Heart's Despair

"Hope deferred makes the heart sick, but a longing fulfilled is a tree of life." – Proverbs 13:12

REVEALING THE ISSUE

Hope is the heartbeat of faith. It's what keeps us moving forward, believing for better, and trusting that God has a plan for our future. But what happens when hope is delayed? When prayers go unanswered? When expectations are crushed? Proverbs 13:12 tells us that "hope deferred makes the heart sick." This isn't just poetic language—it's a spiritual reality. Prolonged disappointment can lead to discouragement, depression, and even a loss of faith.

Hopelessness often creeps in subtly. It starts with small disappointments that, over time, build into a mindset of despair. The Israelites experienced this in the wilderness. After years of waiting for the Promised Land, they grew weary, complaining against God and doubting His plan. They had seen miracles, yet their prolonged waiting produced frustration and bitterness.

The danger of hopelessness is that it tempts us to settle. When people no longer believe things will change, they lower their expectations, stop praying bold prayers, and compromise in ways they never thought they would. But God is a God of restoration. He reminds us in Jeremiah 29:11, "For I know the plans I have for you, plans to prosper you and not to harm you, plans to give you hope and a future." Even when it feels like nothing is happening, God is still working behind the scenes.

WHAT THE WORD SAYS

"The Lord is near to the brokenhearted and saves those who are crushed in spirit." – Psalm 34:18

"Those who hope in the Lord will renew their strength." – Isaiah 40:31

"We have this hope as an anchor for the soul, firm and secure." – Hebrews 6:19

UPROOTING THE ISSUE

1. **Shift Your Perspective:** Instead of focusing on what hasn't happened, focus on God's faithfulness in the past. He has come through before—He will again.

2. **Guard Your Mind:** Hopelessness is fueled by lies. Replace discouraging thoughts with the truth of God's promises.

3. **Stay in Community:** Isolation breeds despair. Surround yourself with people who will encourage you and remind you of God's goodness.

HEALING PRAYER

Lord, I surrender every disappointment and every deferred hope into Your hands. Heal my heart and renew my spirit. Remind me that You are faithful and that Your timing is perfect. Fill me with hope that comes from You alone, and help me trust that my story is not over. I choose to believe in Your promises. In Jesus' name, Amen.

21

Lust of the Flesh – The Battle for Purity

"For all that is in the world—the lust of the flesh, the lust of the eyes, and the pride of life—is not of the Father but is of the world." – 1 John 2:16

REVEALING THE ISSUE

Lust of the flesh is one of the greatest spiritual battles we face, and it's not just about sexual sin—it's about any craving that dominates the body over the spirit. It's an appetite for things that satisfy the flesh but starve the soul. Whether it's food, sex, addictions, entertainment, or any indulgence that takes control, the enemy uses the desires of our flesh to enslave us. It whispers, "Just this once," while laying a trap to keep us bound.

The lust of the flesh is deceptive because it often feels harmless in the beginning. A small compromise here, an unchecked desire there, until suddenly, what was once an innocent temptation becomes an addiction. This is exactly what happened to Esau—he gave up his birthright for a temporary meal because he let his fleshly hunger control him (Genesis 25:29-34). Instead of valuing the spiritual inheritance God had for him, he surrendered to a passing craving and lived with the regret of his decision.

In today's world, the temptation to gratify the flesh is stronger than ever. Culture promotes indulgence as a form of self-care, telling us, "If it feels good, do it," but the Bible warns that "the mind governed by the flesh is death" (Romans 8:6). Lust of the flesh is never satisfied—it always craves more, leading us deeper into a cycle of indulgence and regret. What seems enjoyable in the moment often leads to destruction, leaving people empty, ashamed, and disconnected from God.

Samson is another example of a man who lost his strength because of his inability to control his flesh. His physical desires led him into the arms of Delilah, and his repeated compromises cost him his power, his vision, and his destiny (Judges 16:19-21). Lust always blinds before it binds—it deceives you into thinking you're in control until you wake up enslaved.

WHAT THE WORD SAYS

"Walk by the Spirit, and you will not gratify the desires of the flesh." – Galatians 5:16

"Put to death therefore whatever belongs to your earthly nature: sexual immorality, impurity, lust, evil desires, and greed, which is idolatry." – Colossians 3:5

"Blessed are the pure in heart, for they will see God." – Matthew 5:8

UPROOTING THE ISSUE

1. **Strengthen Your Spirit:** Fasting, prayer, and consuming God's Word weaken the flesh and strengthen the spirit. When you feed your spirit more than your flesh, your desires start to shift toward the things of God.

2. **Set Boundaries:** Remove yourself from environments and relationships that fuel fleshly temptations. Don't entertain what you're trying to escape.

3. **Run, Don't Negotiate:** Joseph didn't try to reason with Potiphar's wife—he ran (Genesis 39:12). When faced with temptation, don't hesitate; flee. The longer you linger, the harder it is to resist.

HEALING PRAYER

Lord, I ask for strength to overcome the desires of my flesh. Purify my heart, renew my mind, and fill me with a hunger for righteousness. I reject the lies of the enemy that try to entice me, and I surrender my desires to You. Help me walk in holiness and honor You with my body and my thoughts. In Jesus' name, Amen.

22

Hate – The Poison of the Heart

"Anyone who hates a brother or sister is a murderer, and you know that no murderer has eternal life residing in him." – 1 John 3:15

REVEALING THE ISSUE

Hate is a poison that slowly seeps into the heart, hardening it and distancing us from God. It's not always loud and obvious—sometimes, it disguises itself as resentment, bitterness, or deep-seated anger toward someone who has wronged us. It justifies itself through pain, betrayal, and even righteousness, convincing us that holding onto it is our right. But the truth is, hate is a prison—not for the person we resent, but for ourselves. It binds us, blinds us, and slowly chokes out the love of God from within.

The Bible takes hate very seriously. In 1 John 3:15, we are given a sobering warning: "Anyone who hates a brother or sister is a murderer, and you know that no murderer has eternal life residing in him." These words may seem extreme, but they reveal the spiritual reality of hate. When we harbor hate, we are acting in the very nature of the enemy, whose goal is to destroy and divide. Jesus said in John 8:44 that the devil was "a murderer from the beginning," meaning that hatred aligns us with his ways, not God's.

Hatred blinds us to the truth. It distorts our vision and keeps us focused on past pain, perceived injustices, and offenses. When we allow it to take root, it doesn't just affect our emotions—it affects our entire being. It influences how we treat others, how we speak, and how we see ourselves. Hate is toxic, yet so many of us live with it, unaware of how much it's destroying us from the inside out.

WHAT THE WORD SAYS

"But I tell you, love your enemies and pray for those who persecute you." – Matthew 5:44

"Let all bitterness and wrath and anger and clamor and slander be put away from you, along with all malice." – Ephesians 4:31

"Do not be overcome by evil, but overcome evil with good." – Romans 12:21

THE CALL TO FORGIVE AND LOVE

Jesus commands us to love our enemies and pray for those who hurt us. Why? Because love is more powerful than hate. Love is the weapon that dismantles the enemy's strongholds. It is the very nature of God Himself, and it has the power to heal wounds, break chains, and restore relationships.

This doesn't mean that forgiveness is easy. It doesn't mean that we deny the pain we've endured or pretend that wrongs didn't happen. But forgiveness is not about the other person—it's about your freedom. When we choose to love instead of hate, we refuse to let the actions of others define our character or control our future.

Jesus set the ultimate example of love on the cross. As He hung there, beaten, betrayed, and falsely accused, He didn't curse His persecutors—He prayed for them. "Father, forgive them, for they do not know what they are doing" (Luke 23:34). If Jesus could forgive the very people who nailed Him to a cross, how much more should we forgive those who have wronged us?

UPROOTING THE ISSUE

1. **Examine Your Heart:** Ask the Holy Spirit to reveal any areas where hate, bitterness, or resentment have taken root.

2. **Pray for Those Who Hurt You:** It may feel difficult at first, but praying for your enemies softens your heart and shifts your focus to God's love.

3. **Choose Love Daily:** Love is not just an emotion; it's a choice. Treat others with kindness, even when they don't deserve it.

4. **Surrender the Hurt to God:** Let go of the need for revenge or justice and trust God to deal with the situation.

HEALING PRAYER

Father, I surrender every place in my heart where hate, bitterness, and resentment have taken root. I ask for Your help in releasing every offense, every hurt, and every wound that has hardened my heart. Teach me to love as You love, even when it feels impossible. Fill me with Your peace and help me to walk in freedom. In Jesus' name, Amen.

23

Hypocrisy – The Divided Heart

"These people honor me with their lips, but their hearts are far from me." – Matthew 15:8

REVEALING THE ISSUE

Hypocrisy is one of the greatest dangers to our faith. It is the act of appearing holy on the outside while harboring sin, pride, or hidden struggles on the inside. Jesus spoke against hypocrisy more than almost any other sin, particularly when addressing the Pharisees—religious leaders who looked righteous but were spiritually dead.

In Matthew 23:27, Jesus declared, "Woe to you, teachers of the law and Pharisees, you hypocrites! You are like whitewashed tombs, which look beautiful on the outside but on the inside are full of the bones of the dead and everything unclean." This is what hypocrisy does—it makes us look good to others while leaving our hearts far from God.

But hypocrisy isn't just about religion—it can seep into every area of life. It happens when we claim to follow Christ but live no differently than the world. When we speak about righteousness but secretly entertain sin. When we judge others harshly while excusing our own faults. Hypocrisy weakens our witness, damages our relationships, and keeps us from genuine transformation.

One of the greatest dangers of hypocrisy is self-deception. It convinces us that we are fine, that because we go to church, read the Bible, or say the right things, we don't need to examine our hearts. But God sees past the outward image—we cannot fool Him. "The Lord does not look at the things people look at. People look at the outward appearance, but the Lord looks at the heart" (1 Samuel 16:7).

WHAT THE WORD SAYS

"Why do you look at the speck of sawdust in your brother's eye and pay no attention to the plank in your own eye?" – Matthew 7

"Do not merely listen to the word, and so deceive yourselves. Do what it says." – James 1:22

"Whoever claims to love God yet hates a brother or sister is a liar." – 1 John 4:20

BREAKING FREE FROM HYPOCRISY

The key to overcoming hypocrisy is authenticity with God. We must be willing to let God search our hearts and expose anything that doesn't align with His truth. True faith is not about performance—it's about transformation.

We don't have to pretend to be perfect. God is not looking for flawless people; He is looking for surrendered hearts. When we confess our struggles and invite Him to change us, we allow grace to do its work. Jesus doesn't want our empty words—He wants our hearts.

UPROOTING THE ISSUE

1. **Examine Yourself Daily:** Ask, "Am I truly living what I say I believe?"

2. **Be Honest with God:** Confess any areas where you've put on a mask or sought approval over obedience.

3. **Walk in Integrity:** Live the same way in private as you do in public.

4. **Let the Holy Spirit Transform You:** True change comes from within. Surrender every hidden area of your life to God.

HEALING PRAYER

Father, I don't want to just look holy—I want to be truly transformed. Search my heart and remove anything that is not like You. Let my faith be real, my love be sincere, and my life reflect Your truth. Keep me from the trap of hypocrisy and help me walk in honesty and integrity before You. In Jesus' name, Amen.

24

Rebellion – The Heart That Resists God

Scripture Focus:

"For rebellion is as the sin of witchcraft, and stubbornness is as iniquity and idolatry." – 1 Samuel 15:23

REVEALING THE ISSUE

Rebellion is one of the most dangerous conditions of the heart because it is an outright rejection of God's authority. It is the refusal to submit, the prideful posture that says, "I will do things my way." It is the sin that led to the fall of Lucifer (Isaiah 14:12-15) and the disobedience that caused Adam and Eve to be driven from the Garden (Genesis 3). Rebellion is more than just defying rules—it is a hardened heart that resists correction, wisdom, and divine order.

The Bible equates rebellion to witchcraft—why? Because it replaces God's will with self-will. Witchcraft seeks to manipulate, control, and oppose the plans of God, and that's exactly what rebellion does. It takes what God has designed for our good and replaces it with selfish desires and stubborn pride. A rebellious heart rejects wisdom, despises instruction, and makes excuses instead of repenting. This is why King Saul lost his throne—he chose his own way over God's commands and then tried to justify it (1 Samuel 15:22-23).

Rebellion can manifest in many ways:

- A refusal to listen to godly counsel
- A resistance to correction
- A stubborn pride that says, "I don't need God"
- A reckless pursuit of sin despite warnings
- A heart that dishonors parents, leaders, or spiritual authority

The enemy loves a rebellious heart because it isolates us from God and leads to destruction. Proverbs 29:1 warns, "He who is often reproved, yet stiffens his neck, will suddenly be broken beyond healing." Rebellion blinds us to truth and numbs us to conviction, making repentance harder the longer we resist.

WHAT THE WORD SAYS

"There is a way that seems right to a man, but its end is the way of death." – Proverbs 14:12

"The fear of the Lord is the beginning of knowledge, but fools despise wisdom and instruction." – Proverbs 1:7

"If you are willing and obedient, you shall eat the good of the land; but if you refuse and rebel, you shall be devoured by the sword." – Isaiah 1:19-20

God desires obedience, not because He wants to control us, but because He knows obedience leads to blessing and life. Every act of rebellion separates us from the protection of God and makes us vulnerable to the attacks of the enemy. But true freedom is not found in rebellion—it's found in surrender. Jesus Himself, though He was God, chose obedience over rebellion, saying, "Not my will, but Yours be done" (Luke 22:42). If the Son of God submitted to the Father, how much more should we?

UPROOTING THE ISSUE

1. **Recognize the Spirit of Rebellion:** Ask the Holy Spirit to reveal any areas where you've been resisting God's will. Be honest with yourself—are there areas where you refuse correction? Are you rejecting godly counsel?

2. **Repent and Surrender:** Confess rebellion as sin. Lay down your pride and submit your heart fully to God. Repentance is not just feeling bad—it is a decision to turn away from rebellion and walk in obedience.

3. **Seek Accountability:** Rebellion thrives in isolation. Surround yourself with godly mentors, leaders, and friends who will challenge you and encourage your walk in righteousness.

4. **Walk in Humility:** Recognize that God's way is always better. Proverbs 3:5-6 says to trust in the Lord with all your heart and lean not on your own understanding. True wisdom is acknowledging that you don't know everything—but God does.

HEALING PRAYER

Father, I repent for any areas of rebellion in my heart. Forgive me for resisting Your wisdom and choosing my own way. Soften my heart and give me a spirit of humility and obedience. Help me to trust Your will and submit fully to Your plans for my life. Surround me with wise counsel, and give me the strength to walk in Your ways, even when it's hard. I choose to surrender today. In Jesus' name, Amen.

25

Idolatry – When the Heart Worships the Wrong Things

"You shall have no other gods before Me." – Exodus 20:3

REVEALING THE ISSUE

Idolatry is often misunderstood. Many think of ancient statues, golden calves, or temples built to false gods. But in reality, idolatry is much deeper—it's anything that takes the place of God in our hearts. It is not just bowing before a carved image; it is placing anything—money, success, people, social status, relationships, or even our own desires—above God.

God is clear throughout Scripture: He alone is to be worshiped, loved, and obeyed. Yet, idolatry is one of the most common traps of the human heart. Why? Because we are wired to worship. If we don't worship God, we will inevitably worship something or someone else.

The issue of idolatry is not just external—it is a heart problem. Ezekiel 14:3 says, "These men have set up idols in their hearts." That means we don't need a physical idol to be in idolatry—our thoughts, ambitions, and desires can become idols when they take priority over God.

Idolatry sneaks into our lives in ways we don't always recognize. It could be:

• Love of money – Pursuing wealth over righteousness (Matthew 6:24)

• Approval of others – Living for people's validation instead of God's (Galatians 1:10)

• Entertainment & social media – Spending more time consuming content than seeking God

• Relationships – Making a person the center of our identity instead of Christ

• Self-worship – Pride, arrogance, and an obsession with personal success

Anything—even good things—can become an idol if they replace God in our lives. The heart of idolatry is misplaced affection. Instead of loving God first, we chase after other things, believing they will fulfill us. But idols never satisfy. They promise happiness, security, and success, yet they leave us empty and broken.

Idolatry is not just a sin—it is spiritual adultery. God repeatedly compares idolatry to unfaithfulness in a marriage. Just as a husband or wife would be devastated by betrayal, God grieves when we turn our hearts away from Him. In Jeremiah 2:13, He says:

"My people have committed two evils: they have forsaken Me, the fountain of living waters, and hewed out cisterns for themselves, broken cisterns that can hold no water."

This verse reveals the core of idolatry: we reject God, the true source of life, and try to find satisfaction elsewhere. But everything apart from Him is broken—it cannot hold the weight of our souls.

WHAT THE WORD SAYS

"Little children, keep yourselves from idols." – 1 John 5:21

"Those who make them will be like them, and so will all who trust in them." – Psalm 115:8

"For where your treasure is, there your heart will be also." – Matthew 6:21

"No one can serve two masters. Either you will hate the one and love the other, or you will be devoted to the one and despise the other." – Matthew 6:24

The Bible is clear: idolatry is dangerous because it distorts our hearts and leads us away from God. The more we chase after idols, the further we drift from truth, wisdom, and spiritual stability.

UPROOTING THE ISSUE

1. Identify the Idols in Your Life: The first step to overcoming idolatry is recognizing where it exists in your life. Ask yourself:

- What do I spend most of my time thinking about?
- What do I sacrifice the most for?
- What, if taken away, would leave me feeling lost or empty?
- Do I seek God first, or do I only turn to Him when I need something?

Be honest with yourself. Idols hide in plain sight—they often appear as things that seem normal or harmless. But if anything has taken God's place in your heart, it is an idol.

2. Repent and Tear Down the Idols: Once you recognize the idols in your life, the next step is repentance. Tearing down idols isn't easy—it requires intentional effort and realignment of the heart. God told Gideon to tear down the altar of Baal in his family's home before he could be used for His purpose (Judges 6:25-26).

This means you may have to:

- Let go of relationships that pull you away from God
- Change habits that consume your time and distract you from Him
- Remove influences (music, media, people) that lead your heart into compromise

Repentance isn't just about confessing idolatry; it's about turning away from it completely. It's about choosing God over everything else, no matter the cost.

3. Return to Your First Love: Revelation 2:4 warns against losing our first love—God. The best way to overcome idolatry is not just to remove idols but to fill our hearts with the love of Christ.

Ask God to renew your hunger for Him. Make time in His presence a priority. Worship, pray, and meditate on His Word—not out of obligation, but because you desire to know Him deeply. The more you seek Him, the less appealing idols become.

Psalm 16:11 says, "In Your presence there is fullness of joy; at Your right hand are pleasures forevermore." What the world offers is temporary satisfaction, but what God offers is eternal joy.

4. Live for Eternity, Not for Temporary Things: Everything in this world is fading. The money, the fame, the relationships, the material things—none of it will last. But what we do for God's kingdom is eternal.

Colossians 3:2 says, "Set your minds on things above, not on earthly things." A heart free from idolatry is one that focuses on eternal treasures. Instead of chasing after things that perish, seek to please God, serve others, and walk in obedience to His calling.

HEALING PRAYER

Father, I come before You today and ask You to reveal any idols in my life. Show me anything that has taken Your place in my heart. Forgive me for placing my trust, love, or desire in things that do not satisfy. I repent and tear down every idol, surrendering my heart fully to You. Help me to seek You first, to love You above all else, and to live a life that is devoted to Your will. I choose to worship You alone, for You are my only God. In Jesus' name, Amen.

26

Unbelief – The Silent Destroyer of Faith

"And without faith, it is impossible to please God, because anyone who comes to Him must believe that He exists and that He rewards those who earnestly seek Him." – Hebrews 11:6

REVEALING THE ISSUE

Unbelief is one of the most subtle, yet dangerous, conditions of the heart. It is not merely doubt, which can be a momentary struggle—it is a refusal to trust God, a resistance to His truth, and an unwillingness to take Him at His Word. Unbelief is the silent destroyer of faith—it erodes confidence in God's promises and keeps us from experiencing His fullness.

The Bible makes it clear: faith is the foundation of our relationship with God. Without faith, we cannot please Him (Hebrews 11:6). Unbelief, however, does the opposite—it separates us from Him. It blinds us to His power, hinders our prayers, and keeps us from stepping into His will.

Unbelief was at the root of Israel's rebellion in the wilderness. Even after witnessing miracles—the parting of the Red Sea, manna from heaven, water from a rock—Israel still doubted God's ability to bring them into the Promised Land. Because of their unbelief, an entire generation missed out on God's promise

(Numbers 14:11-23). Their hearts were hardened, not because God failed them, but because they refused to trust Him.

Unbelief doesn't always show up as outright rebellion—it often hides in excuses like:

- "I know God can, but will He do it for me?"
- "I've prayed, but nothing has changed—maybe He's not listening."
- "What if I trust God and things don't work out?"
- "This situation is too big—even for God."

These thoughts might seem harmless, but they poison faith and lead to spiritual paralysis. When we entertain unbelief, we become hesitant, fearful, and double-minded. Instead of walking boldly in faith, we remain stuck—questioning, analyzing, and second-guessing God's plans for our lives.

WHAT THE WORD SAYS

"Jesus said to him, 'If you can believe, all things are possible for the one who believes.'" – Mark 9:23

"Because of their unbelief, He did not do many mighty works there." – Matthew 13:58

"But when you ask, you must believe and not doubt, because the one who doubts is like a wave of the sea, blown and tossed by the wind." – James 1:6

Unbelief limits what God can do in our lives. In Matthew 13:58, Jesus was in His hometown, but because of their unbelief, He did not perform many miracles there. Not because He wasn't able—but because faith is the key that unlocks God's power.

When we believe, we make room for the miraculous. When we doubt, we build barriers to receiving from God. This is why Jesus constantly emphasized faith in His ministry. He healed the sick, raised the dead, and performed wonders—not just because He had power, but because people believed in His power.

UPROOTING THE ISSUE

1. Identify the Root of Unbelief: Unbelief doesn't appear out of nowhere—it is often the result of past disappointments, unanswered prayers, or relying too much on human reasoning. Ask yourself:

- Have I stopped expecting God to move in my life?
- Do I trust God fully, or do I try to control outcomes?
- Have past failures made me hesitant to believe again?

Being honest about your struggle with unbelief is the first step toward overcoming it. God is not intimidated by your doubts—He just wants you to bring them to Him.

2. Feed Your Faith with the Word of God : Romans 10:17 says, "Faith comes by hearing, and hearing by the Word of God." That means unbelief shrinks when we immerse ourselves in Scripture. The more we hear and declare God's Word, the stronger our faith becomes.

- If you struggle to believe God will provide, meditate on Philippians 4:19 ("My God will supply all your needs.")
- If you doubt His love, hold onto Romans 8:38-39 ("Nothing can separate us from His love.")
- If you're afraid of failure, stand on Joshua 1:9 ("Be strong and courageous, for the Lord your God is with you.")

Faith grows when we speak, hear, and apply the truth of God's Word.

3. Repent and Ask God to Strengthen Your Faith: Unbelief is a heart issue that needs to be surrendered to God. Mark 9:24 tells the story of a man who wanted healing for his son but struggled with doubt. He cried out to Jesus, "Lord, I believe; help my unbelief!"

This is a powerful prayer! It acknowledges faith while also admitting the need for God's help. If you're struggling with unbelief, ask God to increase your faith. He is not looking for perfection—He is looking for a willing heart.

4. Surround Yourself with Faith-Filled People: Faith is contagious. If you arc constantly around negative, doubtful people, their mindset will influence yours. But when you surround yourself with people who truly believe in God's power, your faith will grow.

Find a strong faith community, listen to powerful testimonies, and align yourself with those who walk by faith, not by sight (2 Corinthians 5:7).

5. Take Action—Step Out in Faith: Unbelief thrives in inaction. The more you hesitate, the more you strengthen doubt. But faith is active. It requires movement, trust, and boldness.

- Pray boldly – Speak to mountains, expecting them to move (Mark 11:23).
- Worship through uncertainty – Praise God even when you don't see the answer yet.
- Obey God's leading – Take the first step, even if you don't have the full picture.

Faith is like a muscle—the more you use it, the stronger it gets. The enemy wants you to wait until you "feel ready," but the truth is: you will never feel ready. You must choose to trust God even when you don't have all the answers.

HEALING PRAYER

Father, I come before You with a humble heart, asking You to reveal and remove any unbelief in my life. Forgive me for the times I have doubted You, questioned Your plans, or hesitated in faith. Lord, I believe—help my unbelief! Strengthen my heart to trust in Your Word, even when I don't see immediate results. Teach me to stand firm, to speak truth, and to walk by faith and not by sight. I surrender my doubts and fears to You and ask You to fill me with unwavering confidence in Your power. In Jesus' name, Amen.

27

Gloating – The Sin of Rejoicing Over Others' Downfalls

"Do not gloat when your enemy falls; when they stumble, do not let your heart rejoice." – Proverbs 24:17

REVEALING THE ISSUE

Gloating is an issue of the heart that reveals a deeper problem—pride, unforgiveness, and a lack of compassion. It's the feeling of satisfaction or pleasure when someone else fails, especially if that person has wronged us. We justify it by thinking, "They got what they deserved," or, "Finally, justice is served." But at its core, gloating is a form of arrogance that places us in the position of a judge, a role that belongs to God alone.

The Bible warns us against gloating over anyone's downfall, even our enemies. Proverbs 24:17-18 makes this clear: "Do not gloat when your enemy falls; when they stumble, do not let your heart rejoice, or the Lord will see and disapprove and turn His wrath away from them." This scripture shows that God is not pleased when we celebrate the suffering of others, because He desires repentance, not ruin.

The truth is, none of us are without fault. We have all sinned and fallen short of God's glory (Romans 3:23). If God were to judge us as harshly as we judge others, where would we be? Yet, He extends grace, mercy, and patience toward us. So why do we often struggle to do the same for others? Gloating is an indicator that our hearts need more of God's love and less of our own self-righteousness.

WHAT THE WORD SAYS

"If your enemy is hungry, give him food to eat; if he is thirsty, give him water to drink. In doing this, you will heap burning coals on his head, and the Lord will reward you." – Proverbs 25:21-22

"Bless those who persecute you; bless and do not curse." – Romans 12:14

"For in the same way you judge others, you will be judged, and with the measure you use, it will be measured to you." – Matthew 7:2

THE DANGERS OF GLOATING

Gloating is spiritually dangerous because it reveals a heart that lacks love. It keeps us stuck in bitterness and pride instead of allowing God to work in us and through us.

1. **It Distorts Our Hearts:** Gloating fuels arrogance and makes us think we are better than others. This kind of pride distances us from God. Proverbs 16:18 reminds us, "Pride goes before destruction, a haughty spirit before a fall." If we rejoice at another's downfall, we may find ourselves in a similar situation one day.

2. **It Stifles Compassion:** Jesus calls us to love our enemies (Matthew 5:44), but when we gloat, we do the opposite. Instead of praying for people to turn to God, we cheer for their suffering. This mindset makes us more like the world and less like Christ.

3. **It Blocks Our Own Blessings:** Gloating puts us in opposition to God's character. James 4:6 reminds us that "God opposes the proud but gives grace to the humble." If we want to walk in the fullness of His blessings, we must cultivate humility, not pride.

UPROOTING THE ISSUE

The cure for gloating is a humble heart. When we realize that we, too, are recipients of grace, it becomes easier to extend grace to others. Here's how we can guard our hearts against the temptation to gloat:

1. **Pray for a Heart of Compassion:** Instead of rejoicing when someone falls, pray that they find redemption and healing. Ask God to help you see them through His eyes.

2. **Remember God's Mercy Toward You:** Reflect on times when God spared you from consequences you deserved. If He showed mercy to you, why not desire the same for others?

3. **Bless, Don't Curse:** If you struggle with wanting revenge, replace those feelings with acts of kindness. Speak well of others, even those who have hurt you. Romans 12:21 says, "Do not be overcome by evil, but overcome evil with good."

4. **Leave Justice to God:** God is the ultimate Judge. Instead of taking satisfaction in someone's downfall, trust that God sees everything and will deal with each person according to His wisdom.

HEALING PRAYER

Father, I repent for any time I have rejoiced over someone else's downfall. Forgive me for the pride and lack of love in my heart. Help me to see others as You see them and to extend grace instead of judgment. Remove any bitterness in me and replace it with humility and compassion. Teach me to pray for those who hurt me and trust You with all things. In Jesus' name, Amen.

28

Dishonor – The Heart That Rejects Honor

"Honor everyone. Love the brotherhood. Fear God. Honor the emperor." – 1 Peter 2:17

REVEALING THE ISSUE

Dishonor is a heart posture that rejects respect, authority, and godly order. It's more than just being rude or disrespectful—it is an attitude that refuses to acknowledge value in others and ultimately, refuses to honor God.

In today's culture, dishonor is almost celebrated. We see it in how people speak to one another, how authority figures are treated, and even how individuals dishonor themselves. The idea of "doing whatever I want" has replaced the biblical principle of honor, leading to broken relationships, rebellion, and a culture of entitlement.

Dishonor can manifest in many ways:

- Speaking negatively about parents, teachers, or leaders (Exodus 20:12)
- Ignoring godly wisdom and correction (Proverbs 13:1)

- Treating people with disrespect instead of love (Romans 12:10)
- Living without integrity or accountability (Colossians 3:23)

A dishonorable heart doesn't just damage relationships with people—it damages our relationship with God. Jesus faced dishonor in His hometown (Mark 6:4-6), and because of their dishonor, He could not do many miracles there. This shows us that dishonor doesn't just limit relationships—it limits God's power in our lives.

WHAT THE WORD SAYS

"Be devoted to one another in love. Honor one another above yourselves." – Romans 12:10

"Honor your father and mother"—which is the first commandment with a promise—"so that it may go well with you and that you may enjoy long life on the earth." – Ephesians 6:2-3

"The fear of the Lord is instruction in wisdom, and humility comes before honor." – Proverbs 15:33

Honor is not optional in the Kingdom of God. When we dishonor others, we position ourselves outside of God's will. Honor brings blessings, but dishonor brings consequences.

When Noah's son Ham dishonored his father, he brought a curse upon his descendants (Genesis 9:20-25). When Miriam and Aaron spoke against Moses, Miriam was struck with leprosy (Numbers 12:1-10). When the Israelites dishonored God, they wandered in the wilderness for 40 years (Numbers 14:22-23).

Dishonor carries weighty consequences. God takes it seriously because He is a God of honor, and we are created in His image to reflect it.

UPROOTING THE ISSUE

1. Recognize Where Dishonor Has Taken Root:
Ask yourself:

- Do I speak negatively about people behind their backs?
- Have I dishonored my parents, mentors, or leaders through disobedience or disrespect?
- Do I ignore godly correction and instruction?
- Do I fail to honor God in my daily life—through my words, actions, or choices?

Dishonor often operates in secret, hiding in attitudes of pride, offense, and rebellion. Recognizing it is the first step to breaking free.

2. Choose to Honor, Even When It's Difficult: Honor isn't about agreeing with everything or ignoring when people do wrong—it's about choosing to respect, value, and treat others with dignity, regardless of personal feelings.

- Honor your parents – Even if they weren't perfect, respect their role in your life.
- Honor your leaders – Pray for them, encourage them, and support them in righteousness.

- Honor those around you – Speak life, uplift others, and show kindness.

- Honor God – Put Him first, obey His Word, and live with integrity.

Romans 13:7 says, "Give to everyone what you owe them: If respect, then respect; if honor, then honor." Honor is not just about receiving—it's about giving.

3. Break the Cycle of Dishonor Through Humility: Many times, dishonor comes from pride—thinking we know better, deserve more, or don't need correction. But Proverbs 15:33 reminds us, "Humility comes before honor."

If dishonor has been a pattern in your life, take these steps:

1. **Repent** – Ask God to forgive you for dishonoring others.

2. **Make things right** – If possible, apologize to those you've disrespected.

3. **Seek accountability** – Surround yourself with people who value honor.

4. **Walk in humility** – A teachable spirit leads to wisdom and favor.

Jesus lived a life of ultimate honor—honoring His Father, His mission, and even those who persecuted Him. As followers of Christ, we are called to do the same.

HEALING PRAYER

Father, I repent for any dishonor I have allowed in my heart—toward You, my parents, my leaders, and those around me.

Teach me to walk in humility, to give honor where it is due, and to reflect Your character in every interaction. Help me to see others as You see them, and to value them as You do. Let my words, my actions, and my heart posture reflect the honor that pleases You. In Jesus' name, Amen.

29

Ungenerous – A Heart That Withholds

"One gives freely, yet grows all the richer; another withholds what he should give, and only suffers want." – Proverbs 11:24

REVEALING THE ISSUE

A stingy and ungenerous heart is not just about money—it's about mindset. It's a heart posture that clings tightly to resources, time, and even love, fearing that giving will lead to lack. But the irony of stinginess is that it never produces abundance—it only breeds more scarcity.

God calls us to live open-handed, trusting Him as our Provider. When we operate in fear—believing we don't have enough to give, whether in finances, kindness, or service—we shut ourselves off from God's supernatural provision. The person who hoards what they have is actually living in a state of lack, not abundance.

Stinginess is rooted in fear, pride, and self-reliance rather than faith. It says:

"I have to protect what's mine." (Fear of losing)

"No one has ever helped me, so why should I help others?" (Pride & resentment)

"I earned this; I deserve to keep it all." (Self-reliance)

But generosity is the language of the Kingdom. Jesus Himself was the ultimate giver—laying down His life so we could have eternal riches (2 Corinthians 8:9). A heart that refuses to give is a heart that does not fully trust God.

WHAT THE WORD SAYS

"Each of you should give what you have decided in your heart to give, not reluctantly or under compulsion, for God loves a cheerful giver." – 2 Corinthians 9:7

"Whoever is generous to the poor lends to the Lord, and He will repay him for his deed." – Proverbs 19:17

"Do not neglect to do good and to share what you have, for such sacrifices are pleasing to God." – Hebrews 13:16

God's economy is the opposite of the world's. The world says, "Hold on tightly, take what you can." God says, "Give freely, and you will receive more." The world says, "If you give, you'll have less." God says, "If you give, I will supply all your needs" (Philippians 4:19).

A stingy heart leads to isolation, lack, and spiritual dryness. But a generous heart is like a well that never runs dry, constantly overflowing with joy, provision, and favor.

UPROOTING THE ISSUE

1. Recognize the Root of Stinginess:

Ask yourself:

- Do I struggle to share with others, whether it's money, time, or kindness?
- Do I give reluctantly, fearing I won't have enough?
- Do I view generosity as an obligation instead of an act of worship?

Stinginess often comes from a scarcity mindset—the belief that there isn't enough to go around. But God's kingdom operates on abundance! He is more than enough.

2. Shift from Scarcity to Abundance Thinking: The first step in breaking a stingy heart is renewing your mind. Instead of thinking, "I have to protect what I have," begin to trust God as your source.

- Scarcity says: "If I give, I'll have less."
- Abundance says: "When I give, God multiplies it."
- Scarcity says: "I have to take care of myself."
- Abundance says: "God will take care of me."

Luke 6:38 reminds us, "Give, and it will be given to you. A good measure, pressed down, shaken together and running over, will be poured into your lap."

Generosity doesn't deplete—it multiplies. When we give freely, God provides supernaturally in ways we can't even imagine!

3. Become a Person of Radical Generosity: Breaking stinginess isn't just about money—it's about a lifestyle of giving. Look for ways to be a blessing wherever you go:

- Give Encouragement – Speak life into others.

- Give Your Time – Be present for those in need.
- Give Financially – Support God's work and help the less fortunate.
- Give Your Talents – Use your gifts to serve others.

Proverbs 11:25 declares, "A generous person will prosper; whoever refreshes others will be refreshed." The more you give; the more God refreshes you!

THE REWARD OF GENEROSITY

When we choose to be generous, God rewards us in ways beyond material wealth. He blesses us with:

- Peace & Joy – There is fulfillment in giving.
- Divine Provision – God always takes care of givers (Malachi 3:10).
- Stronger Relationships – Generosity fosters love and connection.
- Spiritual Growth – A giving heart reflects the character of Christ.

HEALING PRAYER

Father, I repent for any areas in my heart where I have been stingy, selfish, or fearful about giving. Teach me to trust You as my Provider and to live with an open hand, knowing that everything I have comes from You. Help me to be generous in all areas of my life—giving freely of my time, my resources, and my love. Transform my heart so that generosity becomes my lifestyle. Thank You for being the ultimate Giver. In Jesus' name, Amen.

30

Self-Righteousness – The Deception of a Proud Heart

"For by grace you have been saved through faith, and this is not your own doing; it is the gift of God, not a result of works, so that no one may boast." – Ephesians 2:8-9

REVEALING THE ISSUE

Self-righteousness is one of the most dangerous and deceptive conditions of the heart. Unlike obvious sins such as lying, stealing, or immorality, self-righteousness operates in stealth mode—convincing us that we're "good enough" on our own. It blinds us to our need for God's grace, making us believe that our own efforts, morality, or religious routines somehow make us superior or more deserving than others. But the truth is, self-righteousness is just as deadly as any sin—it separates us from God.

Jesus confronted this issue constantly, especially with the Pharisees. They were religious leaders who followed all the outward rules, yet their hearts were filled with pride, hypocrisy, and judgment toward others. In Luke 18:9-14, Jesus told the parable of the Pharisee and the tax collector:

- The Pharisee stood in the temple, boasting in his righteousness: "God, I thank you that I am not like other people—robbers, evildoers, adulterers… I fast twice a week and give a tenth of all I get."

- Meanwhile, the tax collector stood at a distance, unable to even lift his eyes to heaven. He beat his chest and cried, "God, have mercy on me, a sinner."

- Jesus declared that the humble tax collector—not the self-righteous Pharisee—was the one justified before God.

Why? Because self-righteousness relies on self. It says, "Look at what I've done! I follow the rules, I go to church, I don't do what they do, so I must be right with God." But salvation isn't earned—it's a gift!

The greatest deception of self-righteousness is that it convinces us we're close to God when in reality, we may be far from Him.

WHAT THE WORD SAYS

"There is a way that seems right to a man, but in the end it leads to death." – Proverbs 14:12

"For all have sinned and fall short of the glory of God." – Romans 3:23

"God opposes the proud but gives grace to the humble." – James 4:6

God is not impressed by religious activity without a surrendered heart. The Pharisees read Scripture, prayed, fasted, tithed—yet Jesus called them "whitewashed tombs" (Matthew 23:27).

Outwardly, they looked righteous, but inside they were spiritually dead.

Self-righteousness fuels pride, judgment, and a critical spirit. It makes us believe that our sin isn't as bad as someone else's, leading us to condemn others instead of loving them. But God doesn't grade sin on a curve—all have fallen short. The standard is not other people—it's Jesus.

UPROOTING THE ISSUE

1. Recognize That Your Righteousness is Not Your Own:

Ask yourself:

- Do I compare my walk with God to others, feeling superior?
- Do I think my good works make me "better" than someone else?
- Do I struggle to acknowledge my own faults but quickly see the flaws in others?

Isaiah 64:6 reminds us that our own righteousness is like filthy rags before God. We can never be "good enough" on our own—that's why we need Jesus!

2. Embrace Humility & Repentance: Self-righteousness is dangerous because it makes repentance seem unnecessary. Why would I repent if I think I'm already good? But true righteousness begins with humility.

Jesus said, "Blessed are the poor in spirit, for theirs is the kingdom of heaven." (Matthew 5:3) Being "poor in spirit" means acknowledging that we are spiritually bankrupt apart from God.

- Repent of any prideful attitudes or comparisons.
- Ask God to give you a heart that grieves over sin—not just in others, but in yourself.
- Pray for a humble and teachable spirit.

The closer you get to Jesus, the more aware you become of your own need for grace.

3. Shift from Legalism to Love: A self-righteous heart is focused on performance instead of relationship. It values rules over grace. But Jesus didn't come to make us religious—He came to restore us into relationship with God.

If your faith feels like a list of do's and don'ts rather than a living connection with Jesus, you may be operating in legalism.

- Instead of focusing on behavior modification, focus on heart transformation.
- Instead of judging others, ask God to help you love them.
- Instead of trying to prove yourself to God, rest in His grace.

Remember: God's love for you isn't based on your performance. It's based on His character.

THE REWARD OF A HUMBLE HEART

When we let go of self-righteousness and embrace humility, we gain:

- Deeper intimacy with God – Pride keeps us at a distance, but humility draws us closer.
- Freedom from judgment – We no longer feel the need to compare ourselves to others.

- A heart that truly loves – Instead of criticizing, we begin to extend grace.
- A joy-filled faith – No longer striving to earn God's love but simply receiving it.

Jesus didn't come for the ones who think they're righteous—He came for the broken, the humble, and those who know they need Him.

HEALING PRAYER

Father, forgive me for any pride or self-righteousness in my heart. I acknowledge that apart from You, I am nothing. Help me to walk in humility, extending grace instead of judgment. Teach me to love others the way You love me. Let my life be a reflection of Your mercy, not my own works. Keep my heart pure, and remind me daily that my righteousness comes from You alone. In Jesus' name, Amen.

Final Thoughts

Guarding Your Heart Is a Lifelong Journey

The journey of guarding your heart is not a one-time lesson, nor is it something you master and move on from—it's a lifelong process. **Every single day, your heart is being shaped by what you allow in, what you meditate on, and what you choose to believe.** That's why Proverbs 4:23 reminds us, *"Above all else, guard your heart, for everything you do flows from it."* The state of your heart determines the course of your life, which is why it must be intentionally cultivated, protected, and surrendered to God.

Throughout this devotional, we've explored the deep and often hidden issues of the heart—**pride, bitterness, unforgiveness, jealousy, rebellion, hypocrisy, and more.** These are not just passing struggles; they are conditions that, if left unchecked, can shape our identity, our relationships, and even our destiny. But just as the heart can be wounded, deceived, and hardened, it can also be **healed, restored, and renewed by the power of God.**

This journey doesn't end with the last page of this book. **Guarding your heart is a lifelong commitment**—one that requires vigilance, humility, and a willingness to let God search you daily. There will be moments when old patterns try to creep back in, when temptations arise, and when your faith is tested. That's why the key is to remain rooted in Christ, consistently surrendering your heart to His refining process. **The Holy Spirit is your guide, convicting you when your heart begins to drift and leading you back to the truth of God's Word.**

Remember, the enemy's strategy is always to target the heart. **If he can corrupt your desires, distort your thoughts, or fill your heart with fear, bitterness, or pride, he can lead you away from God's best.** But you have been given power through Christ to stand firm, to take every thought captive, and to choose faith over fear, love over hate, and truth over deception.

Let this devotional be a starting point—not just something you read, but something you live. **Keep examining your heart. Keep renewing your mind with God's truth. Keep surrendering the broken places to the One who makes all things new.** Stay connected to His presence, surround yourself with people who encourage your spiritual growth, and never stop allowing God to shape you into the person He has called you to be.

Most importantly, **remember that your heart is precious to God.** He created it, He knows its depths, and He is committed to its transformation. Trust Him with it. Give Him access to every corner, and let Him fill it with His love, His wisdom, and His peace. Because when your heart is fully surrendered to God, **everything in your life will begin to align with His purpose.**

Keep guarding it. Keep surrendering it. And keep walking in the abundant life He has for you. **Your heart is worth it.**

In Christ,
Clayborn & Lakeshia Momon

About the Authors

For over 20 years Clayborn and LaKeshia Momon have given of themselves in ministry, serving faithfully within the local Body wherever needed and within their own God-given assignments.

Both functioning under revelatory teaching & prophetic graces, Clay and Keshia are passionate about building God's people, seeing them grow in maturity in the faith, be liberated, ignited and walking boldly in Kingdom authority and power.

In 2022, God instructed Clay & Keshia to launch out and establish Dunamis Regional Ekklesia with a focus on the tri-state region of TN, MS & AR. In 2024, God instructed them to move forward with the planting of Dunamis Memphis, a local fellowship where they serve as senior leaders.

The two have been married for nearly 18 years at the time of this writing and together, they have 4 children and two dogs whom they love dearly.

Clay and Keshia have authored multiple books between them both, with two new releases slate for Summer 2025.

New Book Releases Coming Soon:

*"**Holy Spirit Brain Therapy:** A 21-Day Journey of Replacing Negative Thoughts Patterns with the Truth of God's Word"*

*"**Didn't I Tell You?:** Restoring Biblical Faith & Trust in God for Every Season of Life"*

Made in the USA
Columbia, SC
30 June 2025

60122790R00083